Instructional Strategies and Techniques for Information Professionals

CHANDOS
INFORMATION PROFESSIONAL SERIES

Series Editor: Ruth Rikowski
(email: Rikowskigr@aol.com)

Chandos' new series of books is aimed at the busy information professional. They have been specially commissioned to provide the reader with an authoritative view of current thinking. They are designed to provide easy-to-read and (most importantly) practical coverage of topics that are of interest to librarians and other information professionals. If you would like a full listing of current and forthcoming titles, please visit our web site www.chandospublishing.com or email wp@woodheadpublishing.com or telephone +44(0) 1223 499140.

New authors: New authors: we are always pleased to receive ideas for new titles; if you would like to write a book for Chandos, please contact Glyn Jones on email gjones@chandospublishing.com or telephone number +44(0) 1993 848726.

Bulk orders: some organisations buy a number of copies of our books. If you are interested in doing this, we would be pleased to discuss a discount. Please contact on email wp@woodheadpublishing.com or telephone +44(0) 1223 499140.

Instructional Strategies and Techniques for Information Professionals

Nicole A. Cooke and
Jeffrey J. Teichmann

CP

CHANDOS
PUBLISHING

Oxford Cambridge New Delhi

Chandos Publishing
Hexagon House
Avenue 4
Station lane
Witney
Oxford OX28 4BN
UK
Tel: +44 (0) 1993 484726
Email: info@chandospublishing.com
www.chandospublishing.com
www.chandospublishingonline.com

Chandos Publishing is an imprint of Woodhead Publishing Limited

Woodhead Publishing Limited
80 High Street
Sawston
Cambridge CB22 3HJ
UK
Tel: +44 (0) 1223 499140
www.woodheadpublishing.com

First published in 2012

ISBN: 978-1-84334-643-2 (print)
ISBN: 978-1-78063-295-7 (online)

© N. A. Cooke and J. J. Teichmann, 2012

British Library Cataloguing-in-Publication Data.
A catalogue record for this book is available from the British Library.

Typeset by RefineCatch Ltd, Bungay, Suffolk
Printed in the UK and the USA

Contents

List of figures

Acknowledgements

Both authors have long-standing roots, professional and personal, in New Jersey; we wish to thank the vibrant NJ library community for their advocacy and commitment to professional and continuing education, and outstanding library services. Our development as professional trainers has grown, in part, through our collaboration with this community – we have learned so much from you.

We would also like to thank our libraries and universities (Montclair State University and Rutgers University) for their long-term support of our training, writing, and other professional endeavors.

Finally, we wish to thank the Chandos team for their patience and interest in our expertise, and our families for understanding the time commitments involved in training other library trainers.

How to use this book

When planning a trip there are certain things that need to be decided upon. Where will you go? How will you get to your destination? What will you bring with you? What will you do while you are there?

These are all questions that most people will answer prior to leaving on a trip and the answers may necessitate certain actions be performed. But how these questions will be answered can vary from person to person. Some may search the Internet for travel destinations; others may visit a travel agent; while others may speak with family and friends to learn of different possibilities. Because different methods are used, it is quite possible that different answers may be found, but it is also just as possible that the same answers are reached by different methods. It is also possible that people with similar interests and tastes may reach completely different answers based on their methods of research.

Once the travel destination has been chosen, next steps include deciding how to travel (i.e. by car, plane, train, etc.) and, of course, what to pack. Some of these choices are non-choices – you would not travel short distances by plane, nor could you drive your car to an overseas destination. Similarly, tropical destinations warrant a certain wardrobe while cold climates require warm clothing. Deciding what points of interest to visit during your trip is another choice that may be made prior to the start of the trip, while others may decide where to go during the trip. These choices can be made in a variety of orders and some folks may not choose to make some of these choices until they have actually arrived at their destination.

When we were planning this book, we had a certain destination in mind. Our destination is to convey the novice trainer from the seed of an idea for a training session to the completion of the session. You, as a trainer, have your own destinations in mind and each destination will be unique, depending on the subject of the training and the trainers involved. However, as veteran trainers, we realize there are various ways to reach the destination of a well-planned and executed training session. We also realize that as trainers plan their sessions, they may reach a certain point and decide to – or need to – backtrack and make revisions to their plans. So we present the information in a certain order, following a certain track; but even the best planned training sessions do not always follow the planned track. You may find this book behaves in the same manner. In explaining the details of one area of training it may be necessary to reference information presented in subsequent chapters. Therefore, you may be tempted to read the chapters in a different order depending on your needs. But, remember that we have set our itinerary!

We grouped the information into four sections based on when in the training planning process the actions described will mostly occur. You may also decide you need to refer back to parts of previous chapters to make adjustments to your training plan. This is the true nature of training – it needs to be a fluid plan that can, and will, continually adjust to meet the needs of the trainees. One thing we ask of you, our fellow trainers, is to read through the entire book as a whole before focusing on individual sections and/or chapters. In this manner, you will see the well-planned itinerary of our trip.

Now let's pack our bags and buckle our seatbelts, for we are about to embark on an exciting journey.

Preface

The shelf life of a degree is approximately three years and declining. Maintaining competence and learning new skills must be at the top of every professional's 'To Do' list. It is an ethical responsibility, to be sure, but also one that is pragmatic and critical for career success; 'Continuing professional education is no longer an option, it is a requirement of professional practice' (Weingand, 1999: 201).

Continuing education is necessary for all members of the library's staff, from the director to the librarians, to the support staff, to the student workers. There are always new trends in technology, not to mention in librarianship, that we need to be aware of, and possibly implement into our services. What's the best way to acquire this information? Through training!

It is wonderful to be on the receiving end of new information and innovative ideas, but what happens when it's *your* turn to teach others and impart new information and skills? Whether you're training fellow staff members, training patrons, teaching a class, or presenting at a conference, putting together an effective and interesting program is not a given. In addition to possessing the appropriate content knowledge, presenting and instructing others requires thoughtful consideration, preparation, practice, evaluation, and revision.

Training is a multi-faceted and multi-step process, one that can be wildly successful if you have all of the organizational and logistic details in order. This is where *Instructional Strategies and Techniques for Information Professionals* comes in – designed by two active librarians and professional trainers, the goal of this book is to provide you with the practical tools and tips that will enable you to package your content into a successful training program. Once you know the mechanics of training, and implement some strategies (i.e., co-teaching and active learning exercises), you will indeed be able to deliver effective and interesting instructional sessions. Training is all about practice, practice, and more practice. Let's get started.

Reference

Weingand, D.E. (1999), Describing the elephant: what is continuing professional education? *IFLA Journal,* 26(3), 198–202.

About the authors

Nicole A. Cooke is an instruction librarian and tenured assistant professor at Montclair State University's (NJ) Sprague Library. She holds the MLIS degree from Rutgers University, an M.Ed. in Adult Education from Pennsylvania State University, and is currently an American Library Association Spectrum Doctoral Fellow and doctoral candidate at Rutgers University. Her research and writing interests include LIS distance education and instruction, human information behavior in online settings, the retention and mentoring of minority librarians and LIS doctoral students, and leadership, organizational development and communication in libraries.

She is a frequent reviewer for *Library Journal*, a former column editor for *Public Services Quarterly*, and has published profiles in the African American National Biography project, articles in *College and Research Libraries News* and *The Journal of Library & Information Services in Distance Learning*, the *New Review of Academic Librarianship*, and several book chapters related to information literacy instruction and online education.

Named a 'Mover & Shaker' in 2007 by *Library Journal*, Nicole is professionally active, and has held leadership positions in the Association of College and Research Libraries (ACRL), the Association of Library and Information Science Educators (ALISE), and several New Jersey library organizations. Upon completion of her doctoral degree, Nicole's career plans include more writing, teaching, and research that will enhance the library profession, and benefit the next generations of library practitioners.

The author may be contacted at:
  http://www.nicolecooke.info

Jeffrey J. Teichmann is an Access Services Supervisor at Rutgers University (NJ), Alexander Library. He holds a MLIS degree from Rutgers University. His research interests include staff training and mentoring, and the use patterns of academic libraries. A recent book chapter looked specifically at the outreach programs of academic libraries to first-year student populations.

He is actively involved in training programs in the Rutgers University Libraries and various library systems throughout New Jersey. Jeff draws on 20+ years of experience training staff and library users alike when planning and implementing training programs.

The author may be contacted at:
  jteich@rci.rutgers.edu

Part 1
General overview

To train or not to train?

Abstract: As tempting as it may be to roll up your sleeves and jump right into training and instructing, there are a few tasks that need to be completed in order to properly prepare, customize and implement training content for your specific audience. But even before this, each situation needs to be analyzed to determine if training is the proper course of action. If so, it is quite possible training programs already exist that may fit your needs. These should be studied before new programs are designed.

Key words: audience analysis, demographics, needs assessment, training needs.

When contemplating training or instruction, the first question to ask is, 'Is training necessary in this case?' Is the issue, topic or problem you're trying to address best solved by a memo, a new written policy or maybe a web-based FAQ site? Perhaps a low-tech document will sufficiently and effectively address the issue at hand. But that isn't always the case; there are many situations for which training is definitely in order.

Once you've decided that training is the way to go, the second question to ask is if the training can be outsourced or needs to be conducted in-house. There may be times when another library, library consortium or professional organization will offer a training session that will be effective, and might even encapsulate a content specialty (i.e. grant writing or HTML coding) that is best addressed by someone with specific expertise in that area. Other professional training opportunities can be acquired at conferences and even through online webinars. More and more training sessions are being offered online, which can provide savings in time, travel and expense.

Attending training or instruction sessions, workshops or conferences outside your organization isn't always possible and may not be the best solution for your situation or staff/coworkers. In-house training is cost effective, provides an opportunity to showcase individual talents, facilitates peer learning and collective intelligence, provides a platform for organizational growth and change, and allows a personal touch that can't be achieved by attending training elsewhere. Once you've decided that your issue or goal is best served by in-house training and instruction, you're ready to begin the analysis and planning processes.

As many types of libraries and library constituency groups exist, there are as many types of potential audiences and training needs. Even within same-type libraries, and even within the same library, there will be multiple and diverse information and training needs. Academic libraries are different from public libraries; small libraries are different from large libraries; urban libraries are different from rural libraries; a board of trustees is different from a friends group; and the needs of library staff will be very different from the needs of patrons. So consider who, specifically, will this training target and benefit (Martin, 1976)? Simply identifying library staff or patrons is too broad and will result in having too much, and possibly irrelevant, information to cover.

Before the actual training process can begin, you must succinctly and specifically identify and define your audience (Yeats and Kozlowski, 2003: 262). What part of the staff requires the training? Do the librarians in technical services need to learn the new module in the library automation system? Do the circulation staff need a refresher on customer services skills? Do the student pages need instruction on shelving books? Do your seniors' club members need instruction on how to compose an e-mail?

The more specific the definition of your audience is, the more targeted and customized your training can be. One size does not fit all when it comes to training, and training shouldn't be 'random in – random out' (Nelson et al., 1995: 27). 'To serve your audience well, you must understand who they are and exactly what they do ... There is a wide variation of knowledge, experience, and skills associated with each audience group' (Yeats and Kozlowski, 2003: 262). We will discuss this topic more in Chapter 2.

Once you've identified and specifically defined your target audience, a needs assessment should be conducted. Before you can plan a training session, you need to know precisely what needs are to be addressed; this will shape your entire program and 'set the stage for effective training' (Nelson et al., 1995: 27). Certainly you're aware of some of your audience's need, but you may not know the full extent of their information and training requirements; their needs could be 'both intellectual and geographic' in scope (Govan, 1976: 544), and could be wide and varied, or alternatively very narrow and specialized. The key is to utilize the information you already have and build upon that knowledge base. For example, you know that the young adults in your school library need instruction on how best to utilize the databases pertaining to history; however, on further examination you discover that they specifically need information about the Harlem Renaissance and its impact on the development of New York City in the 1920s. Drilling down to uncover such information will focus your training, allowing you to select just the right resources to demonstrate and tailor your training to the specific needs of your audience.

There are various ways of conducting a needs assessment, some informal and other more formal methods of gathering information. Butler and Howell (1980) offer many ways of ascertaining information and conducting a needs assessment of your audience. You could observe your target group to get a sense of their habits and see what pieces of information they are missing. (For example, have you noticed that your patrons do not use the new self-checkout machine? Maybe it's because they don't know how to work with the equipment. A short training session might be in order.) Other indirect forms of observation included examining desk logs or statistics sheets at public service points. For example, if you notice a high occurrence of the same question being asked (i.e. how do I look for an article the library doesn't have?), then you may decide to offer a training session, prepare a quick point-of-need script to deliver to patrons one-on-one, or do a screencast detailing how to fill out the form that can be housed on the library's website.

There will also be instances when the most efficient way to conduct a needs assessment is to query your target audience directly. Surveys (whether in paper or online format) are one way to assess your constituents directly, or focus groups, interviews or town-hall-style forums can be employed to gather opinions, suggestions and specific questions that need to be addressed through training (ibid.). Finally, your organization might consider forming a small advisory group (made up of library staff and/or patrons) that can continually assess and scan for information and training needs.

When compiling the needs of your target training audience, keep in mind the needs of your constituents, and how they mesh with the overall needs and mission of your organization; your activities should not only benefit your audience, but your library (the content-levels framework described in Nelson et al., 1995: 27). Your training endeavors should merge the needs of your community with the professional and technological trends you identify as worthy of passing on and implementing in your library. Finally, when you have successfully identified the needs of your audience, be mindful that *all* of the needs and requests for information may not be able to be addressed in one session. At that point you will need to consider how many training sessions will be required, and how much time these sessions will take. Training sessions should be fun, accessible and effective, which means that information will be sequenced and packaged in such a way that your audience members will not become overwhelmed, overloaded or frustrated (more on this in Chapter 4).

Action plan

To recap, here's your plan, to be completed before you embark on training:

- Determine if training is necessary.
- Determine if training should be outsourced or done in-house.
- Identify your audience.
- Define your audience.
- Conduct a needs assessment/community analysis.
- Begin sketching out your training session(s).

References

Butler, L.M. and Howell, R.E. (1980) *Community Needs Assessment Techniques.* Corvallis, CO: Western Rural Development Center.

Govan, J.F. (1976) Community analysis in an academic environment. *Library Trends*, 24(3), 541–6.

Martin, A.B. (1976) Studying the community: An overview. *Library Trends*, 24(3), 433–40.

Nelson, R.R., Whitener, E.M. and Philcox, H.H. (1995) The assessment of end-user training needs. *Communications of the ACM*, 38(7), 27–39.

Yeats, D. and Kozlowski, P. (2003) Audience analysis and information design: Creating a needs assessment documentation strategy. *Annual Conference – Society for Technical Communication*, 50, 262–7.

2

Whom should we train or instruct?

Abstract: There are many types of audiences who require training, as covered in Chapter 1. Once you've identified your audience, take some time to learn about their specific characteristics; the more you know about your audience, the more equipped you'll be to customize and deliver an effective training session. This chapter provides information about some of the most common types of learners you will see in your library.

Key words: millennials, andragogy, adult learners, learning styles.

There are many types of audiences who require training; as such, good trainers need to be cognizant of the learning styles and preferences of our learners. Once you've identified your audience, take some time to learn about their specific characteristics: the more you know about your audience, the more equipped you'll be to customize and deliver an effective training session.

If you work with youth, particularly in a media center or academic library, chances are you are working with people who are part of the widely discussed Generation Y or the millennial generation (or just millennials). Born in 1982 or later (Kipnis and Childs, 2004: 26), millennials are extremely peer oriented, expect the adults around them to be human, relevant and knowledgeable, and are quick to wonder and/or ask what's in it for them (Manuel, 2002). At this point in time there are few millennials teaching millennials in a library setting; so for those of us older than this demographic, we need to keep in mind that young adults in this age group are very comfortable with technology (in fact they are considered to be digital natives – Considine et al., 2009), and gravitate towards graphics and other visually appealing multimedia resources. Natural multi-taskers, millennials have high expectations of everything, 'expectations bordering on the unrealistic', and a terrific sense of entitlement (Gardner and Eng, 2005: 408). Gardner and Eng (ibid.: 409) also suggest that millennials prefer learning in the evening, and have a one-stop-shopping 'ATM attitude' towards service and information access, preferring to get their information and 'research' from Google and other web portals that they can access 24/7 (ibid.: 415). Children and young adults in school are often faced with imposed queries (Gross, 1999) or graded assignments not of their choosing, and want to get the quickest and easiest information possible – and they want to get it themselves, online.

With these characteristics in mind, and realizing that millennials are less likely to ask for assistance, please know that millennials are interesting, fun, and, once you get their attention, can be the liveliest group you'll have the opportunity to train. Educators, in this case trainers, 'need to acknowledge and respect the skills, attitudes, and knowledge that students bring with them to school and build on those to ensure success' (Considine et al., 2009: 479).

Millennials respond well to humor (Walker, 2006), and prefer to work in groups as opposed to working individually. Finally, customization is key with this group – the more you can tailor the instruction to their specific needs and assignments, the more successful your session will be. For example, if you know that your millennials need to write an exposition paper, work in advance with the instructor to find out what their assignment will be. The last such class I taught required the students to write about issues of gender and racism as represented in horror films. With their assignment in hand, I was able to construct relevant database search examples and select the right resources; when I introduced the session and let them know that I would be working specifically with their class assignment, I was able to get their attention and gain some credibility with the students, as they realized that I was customizing the session to their needs and making the information relevant.

Moving on from the millennials, there are Generation X (those born in 1965–1981; Kipnis and Childs, 2004: 26), baby-boomers and senior citizens. For the purposes of training and instruction in the library setting, it's probably safe to lump these groups loosely together and say that we are now dealing with adult learners. Adult learners are present in all types of libraries, and have the most diverse range of training, instruction and information needs. They arrive at the public library for job search assistance and help with learning and developing new technology skills, and they show up in colleges and universities as re-entry students, graduate students and distance-education learners.

Trainers and instructors working with adult learners should be aware of the principles of andragogy, which essentially sets forth that this group of learners have distinct needs and learning styles. According to American educator and theorist Malcolm Knowles, adult learners need to know the reason for learning something, are partial to experiential learning and need to have a say and some decision-making abilities in their educational processes; their learning should yield some immediate and relevant results, they respond well to information that enables them to solve a problem and respond better to internal (as opposed to external) motivators (Knowles, 1980; Knowles et al., 2005).

Adult learners more often than not have many life experiences, and job and family obligations to manage in addition to trying to learn a new skill or prescribed content, and it is very likely that when you're training them you will be interacting with them in the midst of a long and busy day. Or, as I have on many occasions, you may be dealing with them in a workshop setting, and they may or may not be there of their own accord (i.e. their employer is mandating continuing education). Either way, the trainer's task is to make the instruction as worthwhile and applicable as possible.

According to Cooke (2010: 211), adult learners may be familiar with the resources and information you will be sharing with them, but may not know how to put all the pieces together. Adult learners are prone to techno-stress, are hesitant to ask questions (they don't want to look 'dumb' or uninformed), have fixed mental models of how things work or should be, and are prone to mental barriers and anxiety, especially library anxiety. Trainers need to understand the special learning needs that occur under the sometimes stressful circumstances of adult learners.

Trainers should ask adult learners a lot of questions, to involve them in the co-creation of knowledge and enable them to ask *you* questions, and should provide opportunity for hands-on and tactile experiences. For example, pass books and materials around, break them up into brainstorming groups, or take them on a physical tour of the library so they can learn where the resources are kept. With all of this information in mind, you will be hard pressed to find a more appreciative and excited group of learners: adult learners who put the pieces together, and add to their existing and vast store of knowledge and life experience, are a joy to encounter.

References

Considine, D., Horton, J. and Moorman, G. (2009) Teaching and reading the millennial generation through media literacy. *Journal of Adolescent and Adult Literacy*, 52(6), 471–81.

Cooke, N.A. (2010) Becoming an andragogical librarian: Using library instruction as a tool to combat library anxiety and empower adult learners. *New Review of Academic Librarianship*, 16(2), 208–27.

Gardner, S. and Eng, S. (2005) What students want: Generation Y and the changing function of the academic library. *Portal: Libraries and the Academy*, 5(3), 405–20.

Gross, M. (1999) Imposed queries in the school library media center: A descriptive study. *Library and Information Science Research*, 21(4), 501–21.

Kipnis, D.G. and Childs, G.M. (2004) Educating generation X and generation Y. *Medical Reference Services Quarterly*, 23(4), 25–33.

Knowles, M. (1980) *The Modern Practice of Adult Education: From Pedagogy to Andragogy*. Wilton, Connecticut: Association Press.

Knowles, M., Holton III, E.F. and Swanson, R.A. (2005) *The Adult Learner: The Definitive Classic in Adult Education and Human Resource Development* (6th ed.), Burlington, MA: Elsevier.

Manuel, K. (2002) Teaching information literacy to generation Y at California State University, Hayward. *Journal of Library Administration*, 36(1/2), 195–217.

Walker, B.E. (2006) Using humor in library instruction. *Reference Services Review*, 34(1), 117–28.

3

How should we train or instruct?

Abstract: This chapter discusses the different factors that need to be taken into consideration when deciding what type of venue would best suite your training program. The venue can vary from small to large and from in-person to virtual training. Where the training session takes place is second in importance only to the content and delivery. Attention must be given to choosing the proper location.

Key words: training locations, virtual training, distance training, webinars, Generation X, Generation Y.

Once you have determined that there is an existing need for training, who will need to participate in this training, and your training topics, it is time to determine how to do the training. Certain questions need to be asked and answered before making final decisions about how and where your training sessions take place.

The initial decision to be made is determining how you will present your training content. There are three basic methods: a presentation, a demonstration and a hands-on training session. Of course, each of these methods may be used in a single training session and there are no tried-and-true rules regarding the type of training session and the content, but certain topics and audiences lend themselves well to certain methods.

Next to be decided is whether the training will be held in person or if it is possible to hold it virtually. Again, not all topics or audiences are adaptable to virtual settings, but as the popularity and ease of virtual training grows, it is definitely worth examining the possibility.

Lastly, decisions will need to be made on the type of venue for the training program. In some cases the content will determine the type of venue – presentation with a large audience will require a large auditorium, while a hands-on session in the latest payroll software would require a computer lab facility.

Presentation-style training

When you need to reach a large audience or you have general information to impart to a group, presentationstyle training is usually a wise choice. Presentations are similar to lectures in a large classroom, with little or no opportunity for a question-and-answer period. There is little to no trainer-participant interaction; it is a one-way passage of ideas and information. For this reason it is best to keep the amount of presentation-style training to a minimum in your training sessions to allow for the free flow of ideas and information.

Demonstration-style training

Very similar to presentation-style training, demonstrations will allow for audience interaction with the trainer. Typically used with the introduction of a new software interface or new company procedures, demonstrations will introduce the topic and then look for participant reactions and questions regarding the content. Because of this, the number of participants may be limited per session to allow for greater audience participation.

Hands-on training

As the name implies, hands-on training allows the participant to practice the knowledge gained in the training during the training. In our highly technical age, hands-on training typically involves some sort of new software program or interface, but it could also be used in learning how to operate a new piece of machinery in a factory setting.

Virtual training

Whether due to the expenditure of time or of money, the overall amount of training received by staff has been shrinking each year. However, the amount of virtual training 'attended' by learners currently totals over 30 per cent of training attended (Garrity, 2010). Virtual training can take various forms, from a formal scheduled webinar to informal, short, view-on-demand videos. How best to present the instruction depends on the topic and the number and type of participants.

Certain topics do not lend themselves well to virtual training. Topics requiring hands-on access to computers can be difficult if the learners need to use that same computer to attend the virtual training session. Learners attending webinars with large numbers of attendees may find it hard to participate actively in an interactive webinar and the leader(s) may find it difficult to facilitate the session effectively if questions and comments are coming in at a fast rate. However, if you need to reach a group scattered in various locations, virtual training may be in everyone's best interest. These learners at a distance are often overlooked when planning instructional sessions due to the expense of bringing them to sessions or bringing the sessions to their locations.

Virtual training is also quickly becoming the training of choice for the Generations X and Y, the so-called born-digital generations. These people are tech-savvy and have become accustomed to receiving information instantly on command. They prefer information provided to them at their pace, not at the pace of another. Virtual training in the form of short instructional videos that are web-accessible can solve this need for immediacy and also allow the information to be readily available in the future. Compiling a library of training videos that can be available at any time and viewed repeatedly will create a valuable resource. There are several easy to learn and use screen-capture software programs available as free open source downloads, free trials, or relatively inexpensive purchases. The main idea in producing this type of video is that they are meant to serve as informal alternatives to formal in-person training programs. They do not need to be perfectly polished productions. No one has ever won an Oscar for 'Best Short Training Video', and for good reason.

Virtual training in the form of interactive webinars can take the place of in-person sessions for certain types of instruction. Presentations, demonstrations and Q&A sessions are all examples of instructional methods that will lend themselves well to webinars. Webinars, a combination of the terms web and seminar, have been rapidly gaining popularity in recent years. Most of the leading software vendors – Microsoft, Adobe and Apple – offer some type of webinar software. There are many free trials available for testing the software capabilities and your personal comfort factor with the software before making a purchase. Advantages of webinars include the capability to see who is attending the training (as opposed to having a training video available online), and the ability for interactive dialog between attendees.

Frequently, questions asked and topics raised by one participant in a training program will be of interest to others. Viewing online videos does not allow for this type of interaction to occur, but in a webinar every attendee has the ability to see and respond to questions asked by others attending the program. Webinars would be a poor choice for a less than tech-savvy facilitator and also would not be a good choice for a program trying to reach a group that is extremely widespread geographically. If the possible attendees are from widely varying time zones, this may reduce the number of attendees due to the need to log in at an early or late hour to participate. This can be offset by recording the webinar for viewing by others at a later date, but this does not allow for the interaction of this later audience.

In-person training

Although virtual training is gaining in popularity for both facilitators and participants, in-person training still accounts for a large portion of the training programs presented and attended each year. If you have considered and discarded virtual training as a possibility, there are still certain things that need to be considered in deciding on how to design your program.

First to be considered is the size of your potential audience – does it number in the hundreds or is it well below 50? Programs with a large audience do not lend themselves well to anything but presentations, so if you have to reach a large number of people at the same time or over a short period of time, you will need to use a presentation-style program. However, if you can deliver this training over a period of several weeks, perhaps limiting the number of attendees per session so as to allow for a more interactive program may be a good choice. Lastly, if your potential audience is quite small, a single session might suffice. If this is the case, care must be taken in choosing the date and venue to allow all necessary participants to attend.

In-person training also allows participants to gain hands-on experience while in the presence of the trainers. This experience can prove invaluable when introducing new software programs or similar materials that the participants will be using on a regular basis, but may have little to no experience in using. The ability to get feedback from the trainers and other participants is something that is not possible, or at least not easily possible, in a virtual training session. If your content necessitates hands-on experience for the participants, this does not rule out the possibility of having a portion of the training as a presentation. This is especially true when your potential audience and your content are quite diverse.

Sometimes training is necessary for a large number of employees in an organization, but only a portion of those will need hands-on training on the more in-depth aspects of the system. Examples of this are a new payroll system and a new inter-library loan request and delivery system. All employees will need to know the payroll system to access their own payroll information, but certain employees will need to know how to enter and maintain records. All employees could be shown the overall system in a presentation that would comprise half of the training program. After a break, the payroll supervisors could attend the second half of the program – a hands-on session on entering and maintaining records.

A similar set-up could be implemented for the inter-library loan system, as all library staff will need to know how to use the system to assist users, but only certain employees need to know how to process materials through the system. Again, a two-part program consisting of a presentation portion and a hands-on portion may be the best arrangement.

Mixing virtual and in-person training

As video technology has advanced and become more affordable, the ability to present high-quality real-time presentations has become within the reach of many. It has also become quite easy to stream these presentations to anyone who needs to attend and has an internet connection. In this manner it is possible to mix the two modes of training, virtual and in-person, as never before. A presentation may be attended in person by a main 'host' group, but also virtually attended by many others located hundreds or even thousands of miles apart. These virtual attendees can be just as interactive in the program as the in-person attendees if they have a webcam and microphone to ask or respond to questions during the program. It is also possible to divide the training between virtual and in person if you have decided that the training can be done in two ways, such as a presentation session followed by a hands-on session for certain attendees in set locations.

Now more than ever there are a myriad of choices to be made when planning and implementing training sessions, and the decision of how to train participants is one that deserves careful consideration. The training content needs to be set before being able to consider the different possibilities: if you are unsure of what it is participants will be learning, it is impossible to decide how to train them. From here, while the possibilities may seem endless, one needs to remember who the audience is for the training, and the pieces will begin to fall into place. Lastly, consideration must be given to any special equipment needed by the participants during the training.

While it may seem quite cut and dry on how to best conduct the training, different combinations will work for different topics, audiences and trainers, so it's best to examine all options carefully before settling on a particular type. Also don't be afraid to move outside your comfort zone and into other types of training. It just may rejuvenate your training style as well as your topic.

Useful links

Webinar sites

http://www.gotomeeting.com/fec/
http://www.adobe.com/products/adobeconnect.html
http://www.webex.com/products/web-conferencing.html
http://www.gomeetnow.com/
http://www.microsoft.com/online/office-live-meeting.aspx

Screen recorder sites

http://camstudio.org/
*http://www.microsoft.com/expression/products/EncoderPro_
    Overview.aspx*
http://www.techsmith.com/jing/
http://www.techsmith.com/camtasia/
http://www.adobe.com/products/captivate/

Reference

Garrity, R. (2010) Workforce training for a new generation. *Power Engineering*, 114(**11**), 18.

Part 2
Content

Developing the training plan and content

Abstract: This chapter lays the foundation for establishing the training outline. The outline is a key element for planning any type of training. It determines the content to be delivered in the sessions and how the training will be organized. An outline will allow for sequencing the content in a logical progression. Sample outlines, agendas and scripts are provided.

Key words: content, agenda, exercises, schedule, script.

After the pre-training analysis has been completed, it's time to get down to business and decide what exactly you should cover in your training session(s). The easiest and most efficient way to do this is to create a working document that will evolve into your lesson/training plan. In this plan, you will explicitly determine what information is to be covered (remember, you can't cover everything), how it will be covered, in what order it will be addressed, what objections should be met and how the lesson will be evaluated (covered in Chapter 5).

In an effort not to overwhelm your participants with information, you will need to chunk and sequence your content. Chunking requires you to prioritize your content; since you can't cover everything, what are the three most important concepts or skills that you want your learners to acquire in your time with them? And sequencing will allow you to present your topics in the most logical and memorable fashion. For example, if you were training learners on preparing brunch for a special occasion, you might decide to cover three appetizers in one session and address the preparation of two entrées in a second session. For your purposes, dessert is not a priority, so you will not be covering it in your training session. Having chunked and prioritized your instruction content, you'll want to sequence your sessions: covering shopping-list creation before preparing your supplies and work area. Sequencing is not complicated, but if you have a lot of steps in your instruction, it's easy to skip or forget some; so the more detailed you are in your content planning, the more effective your training session will be.

Let's say that you can comfortably and sufficiently cover three topics in a training session lasting 60–90 minutes; this would include time for you to instruct, time for participants to work in groups or individually, time to regroup and recapitulate the main points, and time for questions and answers. If you have more topics to cover, consider adding another training or instruction session, whether scheduled for another date and time or later on in the day. You might plan back-to-back sessions, but make sure that you schedule a ten- to 15-minute break in between each session, with the second session covering another three topics. This pattern can go on as long as you need in order to cover all the content you need to address. Remember, your training is not only customized to your learners, but to you as the trainer – you need to be comfortable with the content, teaching format and schedule. The authors of this book have regularly taught a four-day residential training program instructing library professionals on how to train. The days were long (often eight to 12 hours), but consisted of numerous sessions, a variety of additional trainers, plenty of breaks and plenty of snacks! It can be done – it just requires careful planning.

Let's think of an example on a smaller scale – you would like to teach your Friends of the Library group how to use the library's word-processing program. The first 60-minute session will cover letter composition, document formatting and saving the document. This class should be scheduled in a computer classroom, to allow for hands-on training, and this time will allow you to provide instruction and give the learners an opportunity to use the software in question. Your session will also allow for an extended question-and-answer period. When the first session is done, give the participants a break (ten to 15 minutes minimum), or perhaps ask them to return to the classroom after lunch (depending on your budget, lunch might be included with the class), the next day, the next week or whatever interval you deem best. The second 60-minute session will begin after the break, and cover converting your document (completed in the first session) into a PDF file and attaching it to an e-mail. If your topics will be increasing in complexity, you don't have to cover three topics – two might suffice.

Once you have a sense of the scope of your training topics and the amount of time you will need to cover all of them, you can address your training plan on a more granular level; for each training session you conduct, you should have objectives in mind and on display for your learners, so you both keep in mind the reasons for the training. So, for example, in the word-processing training scenario, you might decide that your learning objectives/outcomes for the session will consist of the following.

- By the end of the session, learners will be able to *construct* a basic cover letter in response to a job advertisement.

- By the end of the session, learners will be able to *distinguish* the four components of a cover letter.

- By the end of the session, learners will be able to *describe* the process of saving a document to a flash drive.

Objectives are important when planning your training, as they concretize your content, shape your training structure, and give you something observable and measurable to evaluate at the conclusion of your session. If at the end of the session your learners are not able to save their documents to a flash drive, you will have immediate feedback that alerts you to a variety of problems or difficulties with the training content and how it's delivered, or perhaps you need to lengthen your session to encompass the content and the extra questions you did not anticipate. Training and instruction are a cyclical process, and you will always want to tweak and improve your sessions and your delivery methods.

Another important note about creating your objectives: according to classic teaching pedagogy, as described by Bloom (1956), objectives should be formed with action verbs. Using action verbs, such as the italicized terms in the above example, allows the objectives to be measurable. If your learners can describe, demonstrate or explain a concept or skill that you've discussed, it's a good indication that they are receiving, absorbing, and incorporating the information from your training session!

You will be putting all this information into a document (Figure 4.1), and this will serve as your lesson plan, your guide to your training session. Your plan might also include supplemental notes to yourself, such as a training day checklist (do you have everything you need? Figure 4.2), instructions on how to prep the physical classroom and any reminders about real-life examples, questions and anecdotes you may wish to discuss with your learners. If you are planning multiple sessions, your lesson plan might also include a schedule, with explicit timing notes, scheduled breaks, and any scheduled exercises.

In addition to any opportunities for hands-on practice you might provide to your learners, consider incorporating

Figure 4.1 Sample lesson plan

Topic: Evaluating Web Sites

Format: Library Instruction Session – One shot session

Audience: College Freshman

Duration: 50 minutes

Location: 30 seat computer classroom

PURPOSE:	This session, held in the beginning of the students' first semester at the university, will give students the critical thinking skills necessary to select and evaluate quality web sites that can be utilized in their assignment for College Writing 105.
DESCRIPTION:	The session will begin with a brief lecture of how to evaluate web sites, followed by an opportunity for hands-on activity, where they will select and evaluate at least one site and present it to the class.

Brief Lecture (15 min)	
OBJECTIVES:	To demonstrate 5 criteria for evaluating web sites.
ACTIVITIES:	Presentation and Demonstration
Hands-on Session (20 min)	
OBJECTIVES:	By the end of the session, students will be able to critically evaluate a web site and select at least 1 site for inclusion in their assignment.
ACTIVITIES:	Individual work; group work; discussion
Wrap Up (15 min)	
OBJECTIVES:	Students will describe to the class the site(s) they selected and their reasons for doing so.
ACTIVITIES:	Presentation; Group discussion

Materials		
Web evaluation criteria [handout]	Web evaluation PowerPoint presentation	Blank cards for follow-up questions
Flipchart and markers	APA citation format guide [handout]	Pens

Figure 4.2 Sample training day checklist

Room setup	Technology

• Did you reserve the room?
• Do you have access to the key? Or made sure you will have access to the room at least 30 minutes before training begins?
• Is the room set up to your liking?
• Is the room clean?
• Do you have a clear line of sight to all areas of the room?
• Is the room at a comfortable temperature?
• Do you have enough chairs and furniture?
• Do you have all of your props and supplies?
• Do you have all of your handouts and supplemental materials?
  o Flipcharts
  o Markers
  o Worksheets
	• Do you have the necessary passwords for the equipment?
	• Is your computer working?
	• Are all of your files opening?
	• Is the projector working?
	• Are all of your other pieces of equipment up and running?
	  o DVD player
	  o Stereo
	  o Microphone
	• Do you have sound?
	• Do you have working remote controls and other props?

Presentation • Do you have your notes/script? • Do you have search examples prepared?	

exercises and icebreakers into your training. Exercises and icebreakers break up the monotony of the trainer speaking, give the learners an opportunity to interact with one another and give you the opportunity to build and maintain rapport with your learners, which is important for effective training. Icebreakers and exercises can be as simple or elaborate as you like, and you can have multiple occurrences in a training session. Veteran trainer Bob Pike (Pike 1994; Pike and Busse, 1995; Pike and Solemn, 1998; Pike and Solemn, 2000) provides numerous fun examples that can be used in training sessions and customized in line with the scope and timing of your training plan.

An example of a simple icebreaker used by the authors is to have participants introduce themselves: 'Please give your name and institution, and tell the room what you were listening to on your way to today's session.' By just tweaking the standard introduction, we get the participants to share a little bit about themselves and perhaps make some connections with others in the room.

Once all these pieces are in place, it's time to write out your script (Figure 4.3). A script can be your most important training tool; it can provide the basis for PowerPoint or other presentations, and it is something that can be physically held on to throughout your session. The authors recommend that you write out what you want to say in your training session word for word. As you write and rewrite, you are further committing your content to memory and becoming more comfortable with your delivery and presentation flow. The sample script in the figure gives some tips and tricks the authors have found helpful (color coding, large fonts, graphics) in terms of making your words readable and actionable. Having a strong and complete script will enable you to feel prepared and more confident in your presentation. Scripts are especially helpful for long/multiple training sessions, and are comforting to both novice and veteran trainers.

When the script is complete, take a break, and then practice, practice and practice again. You don't have to memorize your script, but the more comfortable you are with your content and all the pieces of your training agenda, the easier and smoother your delivery will be (for an example of a training agenda, see Figure 4.4). Training does not require you to be a professional public speaker, but it does need you to be confident and knowledgeable about your topic; and the more you practice, the more evident this will be to your participants. Rehearse in front of a mirror or a colleague, or even record yourself (via audio or video) – whatever makes you most comfortable and enables you to critique and improve your script and presentation delivery.

Finally, relax and have fun! Your training is going to proceed better than you could even imagine, because you're thoroughly prepared.

Figure 4.3 Sample script (excerpt)

9:30 Welcome and introductions (30 minutes)

Good morning! How are you all today? How did you enjoy/ endure the trip here today [depending on the weather]?

My name is Jeff Teichmann, and I am an access services supervisor for the Rutgers University Libraries. I've been employed there for over 20 years. Currently I supervise 17 full-time employees and about 60–70 part-time employees.

While you know each other and have become a terrific resource and networking group for each other, we are new to your group. Now about you . . . We have a few **questions**.

o Your name and library.
o Tell us one issue that concerns you about documentation and performance evaluations.

How about we have a show of hands so we know how many have unions and how many are civil service?

- Type out what you'd like to say – word for word.
- Make a note of how long each section should last.
- Color coding can be helpful – for example, blue text for what you say to the audience; red text for the questions to be asked; bold black upper-case text for action items. If you have a second speaker, his/her script could be shown in green text.
- Make your script as graphic or visual as you'd like. Try using large fonts and symbols in addition to color coding.

DISTRIBUTE INDEX CARDS so they can answer the questions (5 mins)

Have students report out to the group and flipchart the responses

10:00   **Continue course introduction (30 mins, second speaker)**

Thanks for that information. I hope that all of you have gotten to know each other and will rely on each other as you progress in supervision. Reaching out to a colleague when stumped on an issue is a time-honored tradition in library administration. We tend to collaborate rather than compete. I hope that this last round-up of names and job responsibilities will help you find a colleague who may hit the same issues and challenges as you do in your position.

Before we get into our topic, I would like to cover a few ground rules.

PPT SLIDES 1–5

First, if we cover a topic that you spent a lot of time on, and redoing it would be superfluous, please stop us, and we can move on.

Second, if you have a question, raise your hand and let us know. We don't want to lose the question when the topic moves on. However, if it's a topic we think may be beyond our scope today, or isn't broadly relevant to most of you, we may decide to 'park' your question and circle back to you during a break or after the session. We'll only do this in the interest of staying on track and keeping the discussion focused and meaningful.

Third, take care of yourself. If you need to get up, please do so. If you need to leave the room, please do so, but we would appreciate it if you would come back. Please try to refrain from using your phones for calls or texts when we're in session.

Fourth, what we say is confidential. Some of our stories do not reflect well on our institutions or on us. Therefore, what we say here stays here.

Fifth, have fun!

We will take a break in the morning and have lunch at about noon. Our afternoon break will depend upon how we are moving forward.

(Continued)

Figure 4.3 Sample script (excerpt) *(Continued)*

 HANDOUT p. 3 and PPT SLIDE 6

Today we are addressing **personnel documentation and evaluation**. Our **goals** for today's session are that you will:

o   recognize good listening skills
o   identify 'good' and 'bad' documentation situations
o   realize that performance evaluation is a year-round process and is based on goals and standards
o   tell others how to document and evaluate correctly.

Most of us think of documentation and evaluation only when dealing with a 'problem employee'. However, documentation and evaluation can and should be used to praise/encourage/ acknowledge a good employee as well. Using documentation and evaluation to promote positive behavior is a very good way to develop your staff and your direct reports.

- This is the end of the excerpt.
- You would proceed in this manner for your entire session.
- Depending on the duration of your session and the depth of information coverage, and inclusion of activities, group work, etc., you could easily have a script of 20+ pages.
- Remember, the script is your guide – use it as you are comfortable. You can read from it, or you can speak extemporaneously, using the script to keep you on task and remind you of your talking points.

Figure 4.4 Sample training agenda

Supervisors' Workshop
Session 2: Personnel Documentation & Evaluation
County Library, West Branch
April 12, 2010

- This workshop has two trainers, indicated by initials.
- This agenda is for the trainers, but you could have one for the participants as well, packaged with any other handouts and materials they will need throughout the session.

Working Agenda

9:30am - NC and JT

Welcome and introductions (for our information)

- Your name and library
- One issue that concerns you about documentation and performance evaluations

10am - NC

Today's Goals
Communicating in the Workplace

10:15am - JT

Performance Issues

- Conduct/behaviors and ethics
- Performance/Production
- Causes

- Be sure to schedule in your breaks, lunch, and any additional exercises or activities.

10:40am – BREAK

10:55am - NC

Progressive Discipline in the Workplace
Documenting Behavior

12-1pm – LUNCH

1pm - JT

Performance Evaluations – Overview

1:30pm - JT

Setting Performance Standards

2:15pm - JT

The Performance Evaluation Process

3pm - JT

Overcoming Common Pitfalls
Civil Service and Union Considerations

3:30pm – NC and JT

Evaluations/Adjourn

Useful links and further reading

Resource websites

AskERIC – *http://askeric.org/Virtual/Lessons/*

Learning exercises – *http://www.merlot.org/merlot/assignments. htm?sort.property=dateCreated*

Lesson plans for adults – *http://adulted.about.com/od/ teachers/a/coursedesign.htm*

Lesson plans and teaching activities – *http://www.ala.org/ ala/mgrps/divs/acrl/about/sections/ebss/cimc/lessonplans/ lessonplans.cfm*

Library lesson plans – *http://sites.google.com/site/cwlibraries/*

Standards for the 21st-Century Learner Lesson Plan Database – *http://www.ala.org/ala/mgrps/divs/aaslguidelinesandstandards/ lessonplandatabaselessonplandb.cfm*

Further reading

Anderson, L.W., Krathwohl, D. and Airasian, P.W. (Eds) (2001) *A Taxonomy for Learning, Teaching, and Assessing: A Revision of Bloom's Taxonomy of Educational Objectives*. New York: Longman.

Seels, B. and Glasgow, Z. (1998) *Making Instructional Design Decisions* (2nd edn). Upper Saddle River, NJ: Merrill.

References

Bloom, B.S. (1956) *Taxonomy of Educational Objectives, Handbook 1: Cognitive Domain*. Boston, MA: Addison Wesley Publishing Company.

Pike, B. (1994) *Dynamic Openers and Energizers*. Minneapolis, MN: Lakewood Publications.

Pike, B. and Solemn, L. (2000) *50 Creative Training Openers and Energizers*. Indianapolis, IN: Pfeiffer.

Pike, B. and Solemn, L. (1998) *50 Creative Training Closers: Innovative Ways to End Your Training with Impact!* Indianapolis, IN: Pfeiffer.

Pike, B. and Busse, C. (1995) *101 Games for Trainers: A Collection of the Best Activities from Creative Training Techniques Newsletter*. Amherst, MA: Human Resource Development Press.

5

Evaluating your training plan and content

Abstract: This chapter discusses the need to evaluate training programs. Evaluating is an essential part of any training session, but it is frequently overlooked or not given sufficient attention. Even experienced trainers often decide upon a method of evaluation after the design phase of the training sessions is completed. Different levels and methods of evaluation are presented and their various merits are discussed.

Key words: evaluation, reaction, learning, behavior, results, predictive evaluation.

Why evaluate? Time was spent discussing the need and grounds for the training with managers. The lessons have been well planned and executed to perfection. The participants were engaged, they asked all the right questions and grasped all the concepts – or did they? How will you know for sure? You must perform some sort of evaluation process.

Proper evaluation, like proper training, takes time and effort. From the initial planning phases, how you plan to evaluate the training program needs to be a part of every step taken and every decision made. The decision to provide training is one that represents a large investment: not only an investment made in the employees who attend the program, but for programs designed and executed by in-house staff, there is also a large investment of staff time. Managers and CEOs need to see a positive return on these investments. In the past this was a simple process. Employees were sent to training and success was measured by how many employees attended and how many hours of training were attended overall. This is no longer the case, as managers and their seniors want to 'see' the results of their investments. They want evidence of the employees putting the lessons learned in the training into action in the workplace. They want to see their employee training programs making a positive impact on their organizations. The proof they desire can be provided through the tool of evaluation.

Four levels of evaluation

Since they were first introduced over 50 years ago, Kirkpatrick's four levels of evaluation (Kirkpatrick, 1959a, 1959b, 1960a, 1960b) have become the standard in evaluative methods and measures for instructional programs the world over. One might think that after such a long period of time these methods would become outdated, but that is hardly the case. Perhaps this is because the concepts themselves are basic and easily adaptable to any type of training session. The first two levels, reaction and learning, are the most used and therefore most popular methods of program evaluation. These two levels measure participants' initial responses to the training and their thoughts on what they learned. But for a program to be fully evaluated, all levels should be addressed, so the third and fourth levels, behavior and results, must also be examined.

Evaluations that measure participants' reactions to training sessions are often referred to as 'smile sheets', since they rarely deal with any subject in depth and most often responses are positive as the participants are fresh from the training and flush with positive ideas about what they have just learned. Reaction-level evaluations frequently cover the broad topics of facilities, food, program contents and participants' perception of their increased knowledge of the subject. Typically a rating scale is assigned to the facility, food and program content questions, with a range from highly satisfied to highly dissatisfied, while the participants' subject knowledge might range from very knowledgeable to not knowledgeable, or expert to novice. Space should be available for participants to enter comments freely on every topic. These forms are best completed by participants while they are still at the program rather than allowing them to take the forms away with a promise to return them, or sending them to the participants after the training is completed. It is best to hand out the evaluation forms just prior to the last part of the training, possibly the 'review of the day's events' portion. Often, participants tend to rush through evaluation forms because they are eager to finish and be on their way. By having them complete the forms prior to the final portion you are removing the incentive to rush through the task and will increase the chances of participants completing the 'free comments' areas. Links to sample forms are provided in the 'Useful links' section at the end of this chapter.

Measuring a participant's level of learning is a difficult task, for it is necessary to ask the participant to self-evaluate the increase in knowledge of the topics. This can be done by asking participants to rate their level of understanding of the topics prior to and after the sessions in a section of the evaluation sheet handed out at the end of the session. It can also be done by actually testing them before the sessions and again afterwards. Tests can either be in a written form or a test of performing a task if this type of testing fits in better with the topic of the training session. When sessions involve teaching a new task, a pre-test would not be appropriate. When evaluating participants' level of learning, it is also helpful if you can use a control group as a comparison. While this might sound difficult, perhaps not all employees need to undergo the training at the same time. Employees who have not received the training could provide the control group. Participants' reaction and learning levels are often evaluated together. A sample evaluation sheet to measure reaction and learning is shown in Figure 5.1.

Figure 5.1   Sample training session evaluation form

Training Session Evaluation Form

Date: _____   **Trainer(s):** _____

Session title: _____   _____

Rate the <u>QUALITY</u> of each factor listed below, using the following scale:
- (NA) = Not Applicable   (3) = Satisfactory
- (1) = Unacceptable   (4) = Good
- (2) = Needs Improvement   (5) = Excellent

TRAINING MATERIALS	RATING	COMMENTS
Audio/Visual materials		
Participant handouts		
CONTENT	**RATING**	**COMMENTS**
Areas covered		
Depth of material		
Examples used		
TRAINERS	**RATING**	**COMMENTS**
Delivery methods		
Knowledge of subject		
Answered questions		

Rate the PACE/TIMING using (F) = Fast, (S) = Slow, (JR) = Just Right

TIMING	RATING	COMMENTS
Pace/timing of the program		

For each of the areas covered by the course, indicate:

▸ How much you knew about the areas **BEFORE** the course.

▸ How much you know **NOW** about the area.

▸ How **VALUABLE** you think having the knowledge/skill in the area will be to you.

Assign a rating of 0 to 9 for each of the three questions, using the scale below.

0	1 2 3	4 5 6	7 8 9
Nothing/No Value	A Little	Some	A Lot

KNEW BEFORE	KNOW NOW	COURSE AREA	VALUE
		1. **Patron Records** • Registering patrons • Acceptable vs. unacceptable IDs • Address changes	
		2. **Item Records** • Record navigation • Barcode problems	
		3. **Confidentiality/Disability Issues** • SSN alternatives • Confidentiality of patron records • Disability services	
		4. **Collection Management** • CS-User • Missing books • Moldy, wet books	
		5. **Library Delivery Service (LDS)** • Four types of holds	
		6. **Billing** • Display of paid vs. unpaid vs. all • Academic holds	

(Continued)

Figure 5.1	Sample training session evaluation form *(Continued)*

		7. **Reserve** • Electronic and photocopies on single record • How to use e-reserve	
		8. **Buildings – Security and Maintenance** • Incident reports • Maintenance issues	

Would you be interested in future training sessions that would provide in-depth knowledge of other Circulation services procedures?
For example – LDS procedures, Reserve procedures, or overview of Technical Services?

YES   **NO**

Suggestions:

The other levels of evaluation, behavior and results are not used as often as the first two levels, for they must be measured at a later date, and most times trainers are looking for instant reactions and results to pass on to their superiors, or, in the case of paid consultants, their clients. However, these two measures could be said to be the most important, because they are measuring the more permanent changes brought about by the training sessions. In the case of behavior, visible and observable changes in participants' work are measured either by querying their supervisors about the desired changes in behavior or by having the trainers observe the participants at work.

Yet changes in behavior are dependent on more than just the training sessions. Kirkpatrick and Kirkpatrick (2006) pointed out that four conditions need to be met for a participant's behavior to change: a desire to change, the knowledge of the desired change and how to accomplish it, the proper climate to achieve the change, and an acknowledgment of, or reward for, changing. The necessity of these conditions makes the interpretation of behavioral-level evaluation difficult, for a negative evaluation could be the result of a poor training session or a failure to meet any or all of these four conditions. If negative results are obtained, further information could be gathered to determine the cause of the failure to change to the desired behavior, and possibly adjustments can be made to allow for the behavior to be changed. Sometimes just letting more time pass will allow the behavior to change.

Frequently there is pressure for the training to be a success or to be completed, so the evaluative process is rushed too soon and not enough time has passed for the changed behavior to become evident. If the conditions have been met, the participants found the training a success and they are aware of the desired change, performing the evaluation at a later date just may bring positive results. To evaluate changes in participant behavior, questions need to be asked of all the participants and also their immediate supervisors. It is important that the same questions are asked of all to maintain a valid sample. Evaluating behavioral changes also benefits from a control group if possible.

Measuring the results of training sessions can be relatively simple or quite complex. The level of difficulty will depend on the results to be measured. The desired results of training need to be determined during the planning phases, and should be jointly decided upon by those requesting the training (i.e. management) and those designing and executing the training. Those attending the training need to be aware of the desired results, but are not involved with the decision. Desired results could be a reduction in workplace accidents for safety training, a reduction in complaints for customer service workshops, or an increase in production and an associated increase in company profits. This type of result may seem relatively straightforward to calculate, but in reality can be complex if the cost to produce (or hire) the training and the cost of having staff attend the training are calculated and placed in a cost–benefit ratio with the increase in profits brought about by the training.

Whatever the desired results, sufficient time must elapse after the training before measurement or observation takes place. Also, the measurement of the behavior level needs to occur before the measurement of the results level for if the participants have not integrated the lessons learned into their work, the results will be null. The results evaluation is similar to the behavior portion in that sufficient time must be allowed for the change to occur, but here the amount of time is even greater. The results evaluation needs to occur at least two to three months past the behavioral measurement. The support of management is again critical for the desired result: if this support is lacking, the result may be unobtainable. This is why management must play a key role in setting the results of the training session.

With all these types of evaluative tools available, one would think that managers would be overwhelmed with data regarding training sessions. However, according to Phillips and Phillips (2009), what upper-level managers are usually given is the participant's reaction to the training program and, unfortunately, this is actually what the CEOs and managers value least. What managers want to see is how the training affected their organization. For some, money is the bottom line and they want to see how their profit margin has been affected. For others, accolades by their respective industries are highly sought after, and exceptionally trained employees can help earn these accolades.

Yet what all managers seek to determine is the return on their investment in the training, for all training represents an investment. However, most participants who are identified in evaluations as having failed to incorporate the knowledge gained in training into their work say the break down comes from lack of support from above (Wick et al., 2009). Trainers must remain in contact with the training participants and supervisors longer to completely evaluate training sessions and to keep everyone reminded of the commitment to the success of the training and the participants. While this might not be an issue for training designed and executed by staff in-house, for trainers hired for single day sessions, this will increase costs. This could also be problematic if the session is being presented multiple times in quick succession, because if the evaluations indicate that adjustments need to be made, multiple sessions will have been presented before the adjustment can be made.

One possible solution to the question of the success of training sessions is a new idea being promoted by Dave Basarab – predictive evaluation (Basarab, 2011). Basarab is an admitted supporter of the Kirkpatrick evaluation levels, and the key areas of predictive evaluation – intention, adoption and impact – are similar. The main difference is the level of involvement of participants and managers in planning the training. Here they are deciding upon and committing to the outcomes of the training in the initial planning stages, and therefore have a higher stake in the successful outcome, which in turn leads to a positive or successful level of impact on the organization. Basarab's method does not diminish the need for evaluation; if anything it strengthens the participants' desire to evaluate the session, and as comments are integrated into the training plan and sessions, the sessions and the organization flourish.

Online training sessions also must include evaluation to be completely effective. As e-learning is still new to many participants, getting their initial reaction to the sessions is important. Also important is their reaction to the design and presentation of the program and any software problems encountered as these need to be corrected before future sessions take place. The question would be how to go about evaluations, conventional means of handing out and collecting forms is not possible so other means must be employed. Many courseware programs have the ability to create and post quizzes which could be used in training sessions where it is necessary to have pre- and post-testing of the participants. Most systems have the ability to create threaded discussions where evaluative questions could be posed for participants to answer. If this is not available, there are online survey websites where you can set up a free account and create a short survey that can serve as an evaluative tool.

Still another method would be to have a form available for downloading that participants could complete and then upload for the trainers to view. Later evaluations to measure behavior and results would also need to take place virtually. Some courseware systems have areas set aside for different classes and also the ability to set up email lists based on the registration lists. These could be used to contact the participants and ask them to begin discussions regarding how successful they have been integrating the concepts from the training. By interacting in this manner they may also serve as a resource to each other if some are having problems integrating the concepts. Bonds initially formed in the course can be strengthened and new bonds formed. The key to generating an open dialog is to promise complete confidentiality. While this must be a part of any type of training done, it needs to be reiterated here so participants will feel comfortable discussing their progress. Remember – most failures to successfully implement the concepts learned in training can be traced back to managers and supervisors.

Participants may fear retribution if they discuss lack of support from above, especially when this is in a written format and attributable to individuals. There are ways to allow for anonymity, but in this type of virtual venue there's no way around the need for the written word. Allowing users to choose their own user names and set their own passwords will go far to ease worried minds.

There are other methods to remain in contact with training participants from online sessions and at the same time be able to evaluate the behavior and results of the session. It is possible to use various social media formats such as Twitter and Facebook to remain in contact with the participants and also allow for them to quickly post messages of successful integration of the concepts or pleas for assistance (Trontin, 2011). Wikis and blogs are also possible formats to continue the discussion. The means of remaining in contact with the participants are not important; what is important is to keep dialog going and a means available for people to post their 'Aha! moment' when everything clicked into place. These methods can also be used for training sessions that have been held in person.

As discussed throughout this chapter, there are various means and methods of evaluating training sessions. What is truly important is not the method of evaluation or when evaluation takes place, but it is how the evaluative process is designed into the training. From the initial planning stages, how the sessions will be evaluated needs to be a part of the planning. Results of the evaluations need to be integrated back into the program as much as possible so future sessions will benefit from the evaluations. Levels of formality can range depending on the needs of the session and trainers for the key behind designing the evaluation of the training is to have the participants feel comfortable to honestly evaluate the sessions. Areas to be evaluated can vary as the information that needs to be gathered can vary. While all initial evaluations are of a reactive nature, questions can be targeted to specific areas of interest to the trainers. The same can hold true for the learning, behavior and results. However, it is important that all participants are presented with the same questions so that responses are able to be quantified.

Training occurred because a gap between the current and the desired levels of work was identified by management. Every step in planning the training was like building a bridge to provide participants with a connection between the knowledge gained and the action. This bridging analogy was described by Smith (2008), with the content of the training allowing participants to cross this gap and the evaluation process providing them a bridge to feely return to the training content and revisit the information. Evaluation is a step in training that is frequently forgotten until the last possible moment of planning a training session. However, this could not be further from the truth, as evaluation is one of the most important steps in planning training and should not be taken lightly.

Useful links

Sample evaluation forms websites:

http://www.go2itech.org/HTML/TT06/toolkit/evaluation/forms.html

http://www.serviceleader.org/sites/default/files/file/7%20Workshop%20Questionnaire.pdf

http://www.eduref.org/Virtual/Lessons/Information_Literacy/IFO0200.pdf

http://schools.nycenet.edu/region9/fashindhs/pdfs/consent%20forms/WORKSHOP%20EVALUATION%20FORM.pdf http://www.scribd.com/doc/26509490/Generic-Workshop-Evaluation-Form

Other websites of interest

Dave Barasab's Predictive Evaluation website – *http://www.evaluatetraining.com/*
Survey Monkey – *http://www.surveymonkey.com/*
Zoomerang – *http://www.zoomerang.com/*

References

Basarab, D. (2011) *Predictive Evaluation: Ensuring Training Delivers Business and Organizational Results.* San Francisco, CA: Berrett-Koehler.

Fisher, J.D. and Hill, A. (2005) Workshop evaluation form. *Library Media Connection*, 23(4), 35.

Freifeld, L. (2009) 50 years for four levels. *Training (Minneapolis, Minn.)*, 46(8), 38–9.

Horton, W. (2005) Evaluating E-learning. *Training (Minneapolis, Minn.)*, 42(9), 35–9.

Kirkpatrick D.L. (1959a) Techniques for evaluating training programs. *Journal of ASTD*, 13(12), 3–9.

Kirkpatrick D.L. (1959b) Techniques for evaluating training programs: Part 2—Learning. *Journal of ASTD*, 13(12), 21–6.

Kirkpatrick D.L. (1960a) Techniques for evaluating training programs: Part 3—Behavior. *Journal of ASTD*, 14(2), 13–8.

Kirkpatrick D.L. (1960b) Techniques for evaluating training programs: Part 4—Results. *Journal of ASTD*, 14(2), 28–32.

Kirkpatrick, D. (2010a) 50 years of evaluation. *T+D*, 64(1), 14.

Kirkpatrick, D. (2010b) The four levels are still relevant. *T+D*, 64(9), 16.

Kirkpatrick, D.L. (2008) How to apply Kirkpatrick's four levels of evaluation. *T+D*, 62(12), 28–9.

Kirkpatrick, D.L. and Kirkpatrick, J.D. (2006) *Evaluating Training Programs: The Four Levels* (3rd edn). San Francisco, CA: Berrett-Koehler.

Lopker, G. and Askeland, R. (2009) More than a smile sheet: Using level 1 evaluation effectively. *T+D*, 63(9), 74–5.

Philips, J.J. and Phillips, P.P. (2009) Measuring what matters: How CEOs view learning success. *T+D*, 63(8), 45–9.

Smith, S. (2008) Why follow levels when you can build bridges? *T+D*, 62(9), 58–62.

Trontin, C. (2011) *Using Social Media to Evaluate Training Results*. Retrieved 13 April 2011, from *http://www.trainingmag.com/article/using-social-media-evaluate-training-results*

Wick, C., Pollock, R. and Jefferson, A. (2009) The new finish line for learning. *T+D*, 63(7), 64–9.

Part 3
The nuts and bolts

6

Who will conduct
the training?

Abstract: There are many options and choices available to managers for leaders of training programs. This chapter examines possible choices available to managers for training session leaders. The pros and cons of the different choices are presented. How the training content is delivered can be crucial to the success of the program, so care must be taken in deciding who will be leading the sessions. Lastly, best practices for working with volunteer trainers are discussed.

Key words: volunteers, consultants, coordinators, understudy.

The decision has been made to provide training and the next step would be to decide who will lead the training. These are people who need to be part of the training planning sessions; therefore, it is important that the decision is made early as to who will be leading the sessions. Possible choices for training leaders would include using in-house staff or hiring a training consultant company. There are options within the in-house staffing choice: if you are part of a large organization, you may have a human resources department with a training staff who will help you design and produce your training sessions. Or if you are part of a consortium, it may be possible to recruit trainers from other members of the consortium. Hiring an outside company might appear to be costly, but could prove to be cost effective depending on the type of training, the time needed to plan the sessions and also the time involved with the training itself. The cost of staff hours devoted to the planning must also be taken into account if you are considering hiring outside consultants. Sometimes the cost of staff salaries is more than you would pay an outside company. Whatever the decision, it needs to be made as soon as possible after it has been determined to proceed with training so that the trainers can be part of the planning process.

Using in-house staff as noted above does come with a cost for time spent planning and executing the training sessions, as this is time not spent on other duties and tasks. While there is no set ratio, you must figure on spending approximately five hours in planning and executing for every hour of the training session. This number would be for each staff person involved with the training. For a two-hour session with a planning staff of three, the amount of staff time quickly adds up, and if you do have a budget for training, perhaps using a consultant may be cost effective.

If you are part of a large organization that has a training and development department within the human resources department, it is possible that they already have 'stock' programs that can be customized to your departmental needs and situations. Contact the department staff to inquire about the possibility of customizing training for your department. This is important, because these stock programs usually contain general·case studies that may or may not pertain to the work of your participants. Providing your own case studies based on real-life occurrences in your department helps participants relate to the training content. Being able to make a connection to the training is important for the participants to integrate the training concepts into their work.

If you have decided to use in-house staff to plan and provide the training, deciding who these staff members will be is a task for supervisors and managers familiar with the training process, content, and the possible staff members.

These staff should have prior experience in training and experience in the topic(s) involved with the training. If your training session is being offered to participants outside of your immediate organization, you may want to open up an invitation to staff from the other organizations to serve as trainers and/or planners. This could be done by open invitation via listserv to past participants of the program or done selectively. For a workshop that is longer than a full day, in addition to having multiple trainers, you may wish to have someone to serve as a coordinator. In addition, for this type of program, it is best to have a logistics staff. This process is discussed in the next chapter.

Sometimes these large programs are staffed with people who have volunteered to provide the training. Working with volunteers is very different from working with staff in your organization, or working with the staff of a consulting firm. Volunteers may have numerous commitments, at the very least; they may have commitments to their own organization with deadlines of their own to meet. While this type of situation may seem less than desirable, people who have volunteered to assist in training sessions are already showing a large commitment to the training. They are there of their own accord, on their own time, and therefore have a large stake in wanting to see the program and participants succeed. Problems may arise if the people coordinating the volunteers are not familiar with working with the staff, and oftentimes a volunteer staff in general. The key to working with volunteers is that they need to be treated in the same way as any paid staff member. They should be included in the planning team and be aware of the needs of the program, including training topics and deadlines. Their opinions should be sought and treated with the same respect as anyone else involved with the program. They can be given decision-making responsibilities, but, as with anyone, there must be clear guidelines of how far they may go with their decisions regarding the program.

There is then the question of whether or not volunteers can be 'fired'. If one of the volunteers is at a point that you want to relieve them of their duties, there are a few things to consider: if this was a paid staff member in your organization, would they be fired? Most likely not, so you need to step back and look at the situation with a calmer frame of mind. The program and the relationship between the organizations providing the volunteers must be preserved, so the best course of action would be to determine what this volunteer did not complete and get it completed. The person does need to be spoken with, but this should be done with the same care and respect that you would reserve for any staff member under your supervision. Lastly, if needed, the person could be teamed with others so that work will be completed on time. Volunteers can make or break a program; with the proper guidance, it can be a wonderful and productive relationship.

When you have the luxury of a large training staff for a program, it is good to have understudies for each lead trainer. Putting out a call for staff to lead a training session may not always be as productive as you may hope. Asking for people to serve as understudies or assistants to the lead trainers can sometimes increase the amount of respondents to the call for trainers. Understudies do not need to have prior training experience, but it is helpful if they have some experience in the topic(s) of the sessions. Understudies will plan and practice alongside the lead trainer and only will need to step forward in the event of illness or other emergency. During the session they can serve as assistants, helping out wherever a need arises. In this manner they can gain some experience, and also some confidence, and possibly in the future will serve as lead trainers. Another benefit of a large program with a large number of volunteers is the ability to have co- or team trainers. This concept is discussed in Chapter 8.

For specialized or required training (for example by your insurance company or licensing agency), it is sometimes necessary, or at least in your best interest, to hire a training consultant to run the program. How best to find a company and a program would depend on your individual situation. The best recommendations often come from people you know, so that is the first place to start – by asking your associates. From there you could widen the search to listservs and professional publications. Other places to find recommendations are your local, state, and national professional organizations. Some of these organizations may even provide training at reduced or no cost. This can be very helpful for smaller organizations that do not have training and development departments.

There are two variations of hiring a company to provide in-house training. The first is to hire a company to provide a webinar, or to purchase access to archived webinars, on needed topics. This is usually a fraction of the cost of in-house training and the access can be used multiple times to cover all necessary staff. The other option is to purchase a pre-packaged program from a company or possibly from a professional organization. Here again there will be sizeable cost savings, and once purchased you will be able to use it multiple times. But with this type of training you will need to have staff available to lead the training, so this must be taken into account before purchasing a program or access to a program.

In each case, working with a company does not mean that control of the sessions is completely given over to the company. Don't forget that you are a paying customer of the company and they should be able to accommodate your training needs and desires. Also, don't be afraid to negotiate the terms of the contract if there are portions that are not to your liking or are unnecessary for your organization. In today's economy, training dollars are extremely tight and competition for them is strong. You want to be able to get the most for your money – both in training sessions and the return on the investment dollars, so be sure the final deal is one that is satisfactory to all.

There are quite a few different possibilities to consider when deciding upon who will lead your training session. From working with people inside your own department or those employed by your organization's training and development department, to companies completely separate from your own, each has its own merits and all should be carefully considered when making this decision. When the decision is made, the persons leading the training need to become part of the planning process immediately. Their input on content, methods, evaluation, and venue are valuable and you will not want to have to go back over areas already covered if they have concerns over portions of the program. So bring them on board as soon as possible, get them current with the process thus far and forge ahead from there.

Useful links

American Library Association's list of state and regional library associations – *http://www.ala.org/ala/mgrps/affiliates/ chapters/state/stateregional.cfm*

American Society for Training and Development Education Programs – *http://www.astd.org/content/education/certificate Programs/*

American Management Association – *http://www.amanet.org/*

WebJunction library online community – *http://www.webjunction. org/home*

The logistics of training

Abstract: This chapter discusses the administrative aspects of planning and executing training programs. The importance of having a specific team charged with managing the logistics of your program (managing people and their needs, and the details related to your location and schedule) should not be overlooked, and should be put in place as soon as the decision to train has been made.

Key words: planning, budget development, location, training logistics, staff development, user requirements.

All instructional programs require some form of a logistics team, yet this is an area that is frequently overlooked in the planning process. This team can be comprised of members of the training team, other library staff members, or a combination of both parties. Depending on the length and complexity of the program, the logistics team can consist of a single person or multiple people. There are three main areas that must be handled by the logistics staff – location, people, and administrative tasks.

Choosing the right location

Factors that will influence the location of a training session include the participants, the program itself, and the available budget. When contemplating where to hold your training sessions these factors need to be carefully considered.

The type of program will certainly dictate the kind of location that is needed to host the program. Large lecture-type programs will need a venue with a large lecture hall that has the seating capacity to handle the number of participants expected, while some programs will have a small number of participants and only require a small conference room. Some programs, while having a large number of participants, may also require smaller capacity rooms if the group is breaking out into smaller groups for parts of the program. Lastly, the program content may determine the need for a certain type of facility. For example, if the content involves hands-on training in computer software programs then a computer lab is necessary, while if the program is only an overview of a new program or changes to an existing program, then projecting images of the program for the participants or including screenshots in the program handouts may suffice.

While the number of participants will dictate the size of the room needed, the geographic spread of their home locations, combined with the length of the program, may necessitate overnight accommodation for participants. In most cases this is easily handled by holding the training at a conference center with hotel accommodation, but other possibilities include college or university campuses, retreat centers, and camps. Even without the need for overnight accommodation, it might be necessary to hold a workshop in a large facility because of the number of participants. However, before looking into these types of facilities, it must be determined that the need exists for this type of facility. With a short program (a single day or less) other possibilities include library or university meeting rooms, rental halls, schools, and community rooms.

Once the type of location has been determined it will be necessary to visit prospective locations to tour the facilities. Even if you believe you know the perfect location, it is best to visit multiple facilities to gain the proper perspective of the different possibilities. The simplest way to keep the advantages and disadvantages of the various locations in order is by completing a simple facility checklist. Before visiting facilities, determine what your program will need in a facility and then use the checklist to keep track of the various venues that you visit. A sample program facility checklist is shown in Figure 7.1.

Figure 7.1 Sample program facility checklist

Training Facility Checklist				
	FACILITY A	FACILITY B	FACILITY C	FACILITY D
Seating				
seating capacity				
seating type				
stadium				
tables				
chairs in rows				
table type				
round				
square				
rectangular				
view of presenter				
unobstructed				
partially obstructed				

(Continued)

Figure 7.1 Sample program facility checklist *(Continued)*

seating comments				
Equipment				
projector				
screen				
whiteboard				
smartboard				
microphone				
podium				
presenter workstation				
computer access				
workstations				
laptops				
wireless				
none				
stage				
equipment comments				
Lighting				
Lights				
all must be on				
spotlights				
dimmers				
Windows				

shades/curtains				
morning sun				
afternoon sun				
Glare problems				
lights				
windows				
lighting comments				
Accommodations				
on-site				
off-site				
singles				
doubles				
shared restroom				
accommodation comments				
Food				
set menus				
packages only				
choice				
a la carte				
none				
dietary options				
food comments				

(Continued)

65

Figure 7.1 Sample program facility checklist *(Continued)*

Parking and transportation				
parking on site				
free or permit				
public transport				
rail				
bus				
parking & transport comments				
Handicap accessibility				
building				
parking				
room				
elevator				
restrooms				
comments				

In addition to touring the facilities, it is also necessary to meet the main staff members of the facility, the persons that you will interact with on a regular basis. If you do end up using the facility, these are the people who will be handling your program, so it is important that you are comfortable with them. Another important aspect of the location is described by Pearl Stewart in her article 'Selecting Conference Sites' (Stewart, 2000). Stewart discussed two conferences where some members did not attend due to the location of the conference. In one case the conference was to be held in a state that had recently reversed affirmative action laws, and in the other, the conference hotel had been involved in racial discrimination suits. Each case had very different circumstances, but these cases illustrate the need to have a clause in the contract that allows for it to be voided for certain reasons.

When meeting with representatives of the hotel or conference facilities it is important to understand that you (and your program) are the customers, and the details of the contract must be acceptable before the contract is signed. All facilities will require a deposit that will be non-refundable, so it is necessary to be aware of this before signing a contract. Therefore, it is crucial that your organization understands it may forfeit this deposit money in the event that the program has to be cancelled for a reason outside of your cancellation clause. Another concern is the date the deposit is due to be paid. If you are funding your program completely with registration fees, you will need a secondary source of funding for the deposit or you will need to set the date the deposit is due after the registration closes. However, if your organization has a positive cash flow, you may be able to use other funds for the deposit and reimburse them from your registration fees.

Another important aspect of the contract details is that most clauses in the contract are negotiable. If there is a clause in the contract that is worrisome, or that does not meet your program's needs, ask that it be adjusted to your needs or deleted from the contract. In the current economy, many hotels and conference centers are actively seeking out new contracts and they may be willing to make adjustments if it means being able to earn your business. This is especially true when it comes to the food that may be provided as part of the contract. Many facilities also serve as banquet halls and therefore are used to serving an upscale clientele, but most are willing to scale down the amounts and type of menu at a lower cost if this is agreeable to your program. When discussing menus, remember to discuss options for participants with dietary restrictions, and also be aware of any cost increases that this may cause. Lastly, be sure to make clear to the conference staff that any requests for additional foods or beverages that will result in increased costs to the program must be approved by you before being acted upon.

During the program be sure to touch base daily with the staff representative to discuss any problems, but also to express your level of satisfaction with the food, staff and the facilities in general. When the program is finished, meet with your representative to collect an itemized bill that should be carefully checked before being submitted for payment. If the program went well and you and the participants were pleased with the facility, it might also be prudent to begin negotiations for a contract to repeat the program at a later date. Not only will you save yourself the effort of seeking out and visiting other possible venues, you may be able to secure the same facility at the same or even a lower rate for your future program.

Keeping track of everything does not have to be a nightmare. Spreadsheets will allow you to keep track of registrations, payments, accommodation, and meals required by your program. Sharing your spreadsheets with the conference staff is also a good idea, as you both can refer to the same document when discussing the program. Several conference staff have commented that they like to work using the files of the program logistics staff, as it gives them a better idea of the program staff's perception of how the event will transpire. Spreadsheets can also be used to compare and contrast the pricing of different possible venues. Figure 7.2 provides a sample chart that can be used to keep track of registration

Figure 7.2 Sample program registration list

Program Registration List

#	Name		Address				Email	Library	Payment Info		Housing Restriction	Dietary Restrictions
	Last	First	Street	City	State	Zip			Paid	PO or Check #		
1	Winters	Carol	123 Baker St	Anchor	NJ	12345	cwinters @wiltonlib.org	Wilton Memorial		PO 09845	handicap access	
2	Bastonage	Michael	9475 Haver Rd	Milesberg	NJ	94750	mbaston @unj.edu	Univ of NJ	Y	Check 873		vegetarian
3	Duranger	Ellie	3028 Griffon Dr	Canterby	PA	45932	eldurange @alker.gov	Alker County	Y	Check 3245		
4	Slockner	Frank	213 Brinet St	Lingrind	PA	45233	fsslockner @hendrick.net	Henrick Public		PO 75390	handicap access	vegetarian
5												
6												
7												
8												
9												
10												

Figure 7.3 Sample trainer logistics chart

	Attending	Dates	day 0 Sun. 10/16 Room	day 1 Mon. 10/17 Room	day 1 Lunch	day 1 Dinner	day 2 Tues. 10/18 Room	day 2 Lunch	day 2 Dinner	day 3 Wed 10/19 Lunch	day 0.1 Tues. 10/25 Room	day 4 Wed. 10/26 Lunch
Coordinator	1	10/17–19, 26	1	1	1	1	1	1	1	1		1
Coordinator	2	10/17–19, 26		1	1	1	1	1	1	1		1
Coordinator	3	10/17–19, 26		1	1	1		1	1	1		1
Trainer	1	10/17, 19, & 26			1					1		1
Trainer	2	10/17			1	1						
Trainer	3	10/18						1	1			
Trainer	4	10/19								1		
Trainer	5	10/26										1
Trainer	6	10/19								1		
Trainer	7	10/17–18		1	1	1		1	1			
Trainer	8	10/19								1		
Trainer	9	10/17			1	1						
Trainer	10	10/17–18			1			1				
Trainer	11	10/18						1	1			
Trainer	12	10/19								1		

Trainer	13	10/17						1		
Trainer	14	10/17–19, 26	1		1	1	1	1		1
Trainer	15	10/17–18			1	1	1			
Participants		10/17–19, 26	0	17	17	17	17	17	0	17
Guests					2					
TOTAL			1	22	30	25 / 19	26	25 / 26	0	23
	cost per		$122.50	$122.50	$92.50	$122.50	$83.25	$58.75	$122.50	$67.75
	SUB-TOTALS		$122.50	$2,695.00	$2,775.00	$2,327.50	$2,164.50	$1,527.50	$0.00	$1,558.25

TOTAL	$13,170.25
credit due for having less people at dinner ($32.00 per)	$192.00
TOTAL	$12,978.25

and payments. This chart can also be used to note any dietary or accommodations requests.

Figure 7.3 shows a sample spreadsheet that will be useful to keep track of many different aspects of the program accommodations. First, it can be used to keep track of the trainers and days that they will be in attendance at the program. Accommodation and meals needs for the trainers, participants, and guests can be logged into the spreadsheet easily, calculating not only the numbers needed by day of the program, but also a total cost expended by the number of meals and rooms needed. Any adjustments to the overall cost, such as deductions for lower numbers of attendees at a meal, can also be inserted. This type of spreadsheet will prove invaluable when planning a budget for the program, but also when the time comes to verify the invoices when the program is finished.

Handling people

The logistics staff may also handle all the 'people' tasks that are involved in producing any sort of training program. Shorter programs will not require much in the way of people handling, but a program that requires food and drink and/or overnight accommodations will require a great deal. There will be people with dietary requirements and dietary requests, and possibly different numbers of people for meals on different days. If you are including overnight accommodation, you may have requests for specialty rooms; and if you are having multiple overnights with multiple speakers/trainers, you may need different numbers of rooms each night. Once again, a spreadsheet is a great aid in keeping track of everything.

Another aspect of people handling is managing their complaints. Even with a small group there will be issues to address and problems to solve; increase the size of the group and you will increase the amount of problems. In programs where you are using a hotel or conference center, participants may bring their problems to the attention of the hotel staff, but in reality the participants are *your* customers and it is the *program* that is the customer of the hotel. You and your logistics team must serve as the go-betweens for the participants and the hotel staff otherwise you may not be aware of ongoing problems. These problems may result in poor evaluations of your program, or, even worse, the reputation of your program could suffer greatly over a simple issue that you were completely unaware of at the time.

Another area where the logistics team may work with handling people is working with any volunteers and guest speakers or presenters in the program. Coordinating the work of volunteers takes a careful hand and a watchful eye. While many volunteers can be dedicated individuals, some volunteers for reasons of their own, not for the success of the program. These individuals will need close direction, and this is not possible if you are leading the program. Volunteer position responsibilities need to be spelled out as clearly as you would a paid position description. We have had volunteer trainers show up at the last (and we mean last!) possible moment before their session. In addition, their understudy was also a no-show. We were in the midst of a quick review of our notes, preparing to lead this portion of the program, when in strolled the missing trainer. If we had clearly stated that all trainers for the day's sessions need to be present by 9am, perhaps we would not have had this problem. We learned from this experience and now have descriptive paragraphs for all of the volunteer positions. This also helps people know exactly what they are signing up to do when they step forward as a volunteer.

If your program is fortunate to have guest speakers for certain portions of your program, their arrival and accommodations are best handled by someone not directly involved with presenting a portion of the program. This will allow them to be available to greet the guest and help them get settled without interruption to the program.

Administrative tasks

Administrative tasks are the backbone of any program; without them, or without them performed properly, a program will most certainly collapse. The logistics team may consist of staff members of a single library or organization or be comprised of people from multiple locations. Whatever the composition of the team, it is important to have people working on the administrative tasks who are able to work independently. Public knowledge of a program most often begins with publicity in the form of fliers, newsletter or listserv announcements, or direct mailings which are produced by the administrative arm of the logistics team. Registration materials are also produced and collected by the team. Once again a spreadsheet proves indispensible in keeping registrations and payments straight. The logistics team can also reproduce handouts needed for the program. If this is to be the case, certain conditions must be met so that the materials can be ready in a timely fashion at an affordable cost.

Dates must be set, and all involved need to be cognizant of these dates and adhere to them. The first date would be the deadline for all materials requiring reproduction to be received by the administrative team. The second would be the date by which the handouts need to be completed. Both dates are very important to the success of the program, and they should be mutually agreeable to all parties involved.

Having a key person not able to meet one of these dates could result in incomplete or inaccurate handouts. Another issue of concern with the production of handouts is the cost of their reproduction. Depending on the amount of handouts and the number of participants, the cost of reproducing the handouts can quickly add up, especially if the cost is to be borne by a single entity. Setting a reasonable cost per page in the planning stages will allow the handouts to be completed without animosity.

The financial aspects of the program are also handled by the administrative arm of the logistics team. In the planning stages, a budget must be created that will be followed by the team when tracking the income and expenditures. Creating a budget is a daunting task that many have not previously encountered. However, it can be relatively straightforward if one approaches the task one step at a time. First, all possible costs should be given a line item in a spreadsheet, even if approximate costs cannot be determined for every line item at this time. Any items whose cost can be approximated or is known should have values entered. This will leave you with having to determine some sort of estimated amount for your unknown costs. Frequently, the largest unknown cost will be the cost of the contract for the facility where the program is being held. This cost will become a known cost soon enough, but in the early stages approximate costs can be found by speaking with the staff of short-listed facilities. If one of the costs, such as reproduction of the program handouts, is going to be covered by a sponsor or an administrator of the program, it is still important to list this cost. A separate line negating the cost, on the income portion of the budget, will be present for any costs being covered outside of income from the program. If the program is going to be presented in future years, these costs may not be borne by outside entities, so knowing what the cost was for past years will prove helpful.

Once the approximated costs have been determined, it is time to focus on the income side of the budget. Armed with an approximate total cost, the next step is to determine how these costs will be covered. The most common sources of funding for workshop costs are the administrative budget of the library or information center and the participant registration fees, but another possibility is to apply for a grant to cover all or part of the costs. Grant sources include national and state library associations and private foundations. List all sources of funding as separate line items in the income portion of your budget spreadsheet as shown in Figure 7.4.

Figure 7.4   Sample general budget

Workshop Budget - YEAR

Income			
Organization			
Grants			
Participant fees	X x $Y		
Total Income		$0.00	
Expenditure			
Net		$0.00	

Item	Budgeted	Actual	Difference	Comments
Meeting Rooms				
Hotel Rooms				
Food				
Snacks and Drinks				
Participant/trainer gifts				
Guest speaker				
Misc				
TOTAL	$0.00			

Spreadsheets can also be used to aid the decision-making process to compare and contrast the different possible venues and their associated costs. While it may be difficult to make columns that will provide a direct comparison between each venue it may be possible to make adjustments for the different packages offered. A sample spreadsheet is shown in Figure 7.5.

Oftentimes the cost to the participants of the program is an unknown figure in the initial planning phases. Once the expenses have been determined, it is possible to use spreadsheets such as those in Figure 7.6 to determine the income generated from different possible participant fees. While no program should be planned with a budgeted net income in a negative range, most programs do not have the capability to finish with a large positive income, so the need to set a participant fee as low as possible to cover costs is usually paramount. It is important that it is clear to all involved what will happen to net income after all invoices have been paid. If the program does have a sponsoring organization, most times this amount can be used to offset their contribution. In the case of programs that are fully funded by participant fees, it is important to know where any extra funds will reside after the program ends and who will control them until they are needed again.

Developing the curriculum for instructional programs is a difficult and time-consuming task, as is presenting the material to the participants, but the logistics involved with these programs can be just as daunting. Frequently the area of logistics can be overlooked or underestimated when setting up an instructional or training team. Often the duties are parceled out amongst the trainers, who themselves may already be overburdened with their training load. It cannot be stressed more that these duties need to be assigned to individuals who do not have other duties in the program.

Figure 7.5 Sample workshop venue comparison chart

	Camping Retreat Center			American Conference Center			International Hotel			Comments
	per	x	total	per	x	total	per	x	total	
Meeting Rooms			$0.00	$200.00	2	$400.00	$100.00	4	$400.00	Mostly included costs listed are the only not included
Hotel Rooms			$0.00	$106.00	58	$6,148.00	$122.00	58	$7,076.00	((25 part. + 2 coords) X 2 nights) + 4 for OV trainers
Misc.				$50.00	2	$100.00				podium and mic at dinner
Food	$65.00	120	$7,800.00	$55.00	120	$6,600.00				IH package include breakfast, lunch and break foods
Breakfast	*Package rate includes*			*ACC meeting package includes*			$6.95	30	$417.00	X 2 days
Breaks	*breakfast, lunch, dinner*			*breakfast, lunch, break foods/drinks*			$6.50	30	$780.00	X 4 days
Lunch Type 1	*and the cost of the meeting rooms*			*and the cost of the meeting rooms*			$17.95	30	$2,154.00	X 4 days

Item	Description		Price	Qty	Total	Price	Qty	Total	Notes
Lunch Type 2	Break foods/drinks would still need to be purchased separately.					$1.50	30	$45.00	Fruit added to breakfast @ IH 1st day
Dinner Type 1			$29.95	30	$898.50	$26.95	30	$1,617.00	X 2 days
Dinner Type 2			$29.95	30	$898.50		30	$0.00	X 2 days
Food sub-total		$0.00			$8,397.00			$5,013.00	
Gratuity	Break Foods/ Drinks	$250.00		20%	$1,759.40		20%	$1,082.60	
Server fees								$0.00	Waived by IH
Food Total		$250.00			$10,156.40			$6,095.60	
GRAND TOTAL		$8,050.00			$16,804.40			$13,571.60	

Figure 7.6 Sample detailed budget

Workshop Budget – YEAR

Item	Prior YEAR Actual	YEAR Budgeted	Comments
Meeting Rooms	$300.00	$300.00	
Hotel Rooms	$6,710.04	$7,516.80	*58 rooms @ $120 per + 8% occupancy tax*
Food	$10,221.66	$10,250.00	
Internet @ hotel	$150.00	$150.00	
Screens for meeting rooms	$160.00	$160.00	
Participant/trainer gifts	$767.67	$700.00	
Guest speaker	$1,000.00	$1,000.00	
Handouts	$534.00	$500.00	*paper, copying, toner, etc.*
Misc. training materials	$19.23	$50.00	
Misc	$221.47	$250.00	
TOTAL	$20,084.07	$20,876.80	

Workshop – YEAR				Variance in Participant Fees				
Income		at $400	at $425	at $450	at $475	at $500	at $525
Your Organization		$12,000.00	$12,000.00	$12,000.00	$12,000.00	$12,000.00	$12,000.00
Participant fees	X = 20	$8,000.00	$8,500.00	$9,000.00	$9,500.00	$10,000.00	$10,500.00
Total Income		$20,000.00	$20,500.00	$21,000.00	$21,500.00	$22,000.00	$22,500.00
Estimated Expenditure – Meeting space and food		$18,400.00	$18,400.00	$18,400.00	$18,400.00	$18,400.00	$18,400.00
Estimated Expenditure – other		$2,500.00	$2,500.00	$2,500.00	$2,500.00	$2,500.00	$2,500.00
Net		($900.00)	($400.00)	$100.00	$600.00	$1,100.00	$1,600.00

These individuals will be kept quite busy before, during, and after the program. They need to be organized and have meticulous attention to detail. These individuals need to be informed of the importance of the tasks they are about to undertake as the success of the program rests just as much on them as it does the trainers.

As trainers, we want our programs to be enjoyed by our participants, and the logistics play a large part in the participant's enjoyment of a program. It cannot be stressed enough: pay just as much attention to your program's logistics as you do to your program's content, because the participants sure will. Using the ideas and tools presented here, the work of the logistics team will be organized and professional. Programs that are well organized are successful and receive high praise from their attendees. You want your program remembered for the content and not for the poor quality lunch or temperature extremes, so remember: pay attention to the small details.

Useful links and further reading

Websites

http://www.ala.org/ala/aboutala/offices/wo/woissues/
    washfunding/grants/grants.cfm
http://www.grants.gov/applicants/find_grant_opportunities.
    jsp
http://www.nlm.nih.gov/services/grant_info.html
http://grants.library.wisc.edu/organizations/
    internationalfunding.html
http://www.weitzenegger.de/en/funds.html
http://www.ifla.org/en/funds-grants-awards
http://librarygrants.blogspot.com/

Further reading

Bice-Stephens, W. (2001) Designing a conference – from start to finish. *The Journal of Continuing Education in Nursing*, 32(5), 198–202.

Burkhardt, J.M., MacDonald, M.C. and Rathemacher, A.J. (2001) Blueprint for planning a successful program. *American Libraries*, 32(10), 48–50.

Gray, C. (2009) Conference planning: What does it take? *Idaho Librarian (Online)*.

Leach, L.C. (1994) A planning primer for small associations. *Association Management*, 46(**April**), 83–101.

Treadwell IV, L., and Casper C. (2008) Developing leadership skills for reference librarians: The case for planning a local conference. *The Reference Librarian*, 49(2), 135–48.

Reference

Stewart, P. (2000) Selecting conference sites. *Black Issues in Higher Education*, 17(6), 18–21.

The trainer's toolbox: tips and tricks for making training successful

Abstract: This chapter provides helpful tips and tricks for trainers designed to aid both the novice and seasoned trainer alike. The topics discussed include the merits of team training, to the preparation needed to take your 'show on the road', to training in your home location. Special emphasis is given to the importance of having detailed backup plans and equipment at the ready.

Key words: co-training, checklists, back-up plans, travel, physical needs for training.

Co-teaching

One of the best parts of planning and delivering your own custom training and instruction sessions is that in addition to catering to the specific needs of your audience, there is also ample opportunity to cater to yourself as a trainer. Training gives you the opportunity to showcase your individual talents and expertise, and it also gives you the opportunity to collaborate with other trainers and instructors. Co-training can be an effective way to train, and it can alleviate some of the pressure that can accompany the implementation of a training session.

Cook and Friend (2004) describe co-teaching as an instruction or training scenario in which two or more people agree 'to share instructional responsibility, for a single group of students, primarily in a single classroom or workspace, for specific content, with mutual ownership, pooled resources, and joint accountability' (Villa et al., 2008: 5). Co-teaching, or co-training, is a 'cooperative process' (ibid.: 4) that provides you with a partner with whom you can split the planning and teaching responsibilities of your session or sessions. You and your co-trainer are joint contributors to the training session, from the beginning stages of analyzing your community to creating and structuring the content, up through the evaluation and retooling of the lesson. Co-training can require a bit more work and scheduling when preparing a session, but that work is rewarded during the actual delivery of the session when you have someone in the front of the room with you leading the training event.

Co-training can be especially useful and helpful for novice trainers as it provides an automatic backup and a sense of security, facilitates diversity in the delivery of training content (with regard to voice and perspective), and having a partner can aid in keeping you on time and on task, and aid in answering participant questions. Co-training is equally useful for veteran trainers as well; the authors of this book have been co-trainers for many years and have developed a great working relationship, one that allows us to play off each others' strengths and expertise, and enjoy a great level of comfort when delivering multi-day, multi-lesson training sessions.

Taking your show on the road!

At some point in your career, you may be asked to 'take your show on the road' and train staff in another location. Now this might mean traveling to a facility across town or across the state or across the country, but in each case there are certain preparations you can make to assure that your training will go smoothly.

The first step in your planning would be to determine what you will need to produce the training. The first pass at this list should be completely exhaustive, meaning it should include everything you would need from the participant handouts to the flipcharts and/or projection equipment; even the preferred seating arrangements for the participants. If you have presented this particular training session before, this list should be easy to compile, but for a new session this will take some work. One method that works well for this (and can also be used to determine a rough timing for the session) is to write some quick notes into the margins of the lesson plans or handouts for the session. Notes would include things like flipchart participants' answers to the question, pass out case studies, show a certain website, etc. In this manner you will soon have a list of things that you will need for the session and can divide them into what is going to be provided for you at the training location and what you will need to bring with you.

If at all possible, you should visit the training location to test equipment and to determine if the facility can handle the program. Things to look at/determine would include: seating/room arrangement, lighting, equipment, parking, ease of access, and internet access. A handy checklist for keeping track of everything is provided in Figure 8.1. This is quite similar to the checklist used to compare and contrast facilities when you are shopping for conference facilities. Saving these checklists and sharing them with other trainers is helpful as sometimes it is not possible to make a trip to visit a facility. Making some notes regarding your thoughts on each of the main categories – seating, lighting, parking and transportation, equipment, and handicap accessibility that are specific to your particular workshop and your needs – will be helpful as the workshop date approaches and

Figure 8.1 Sample facility review checklist

Facility Review Checklist		
Facility		
Reviewed by		
Date reviewed		
Seating		Comments
seating capacity		
seating type		
stadium		
tables		
chairs in rows		
table type		
round		
square		
rectangular		
view of presenter		
unobstructed		
partially obstruct		
Equipment		Comments
projector		
screen		
whiteboard		
smartboard		
microphone		
podium		
presenter workstation		

computer access		
workstations		
laptops		
wireless		
none		

Lighting		Comments
Lights		
all must be on		
spotlights		
dimmers		
Windows		
shades/curtains		
morning sun		
afternoon sun		
Glare problems		
lights		
windows		

Parking and transportation		Comments
parking on site		
free or permit		
public transport		
rail		
bus		

Handicap Accessibility		Comments
building		
parking		
room		
elevator		
restrooms		

you are in contact with the facility staff. You want to be sure to speak with the staff member who is in charge of scheduling the rooms when you visit to discuss how other trainers have used the room in the past. Asking their opinion on the best arrangement of the room for your workshop will save you time in considering possible arrangements, and also show deference to their knowledge of the facility.

At this time it is also prudent to discuss with the facility staff what other events are or may be occurring at the same time as your event. In this manner you may avoid possible conflicts with another program. This is mentioned because in our experience we have seen rooms get switched or downsized because the facility decided to, or needed to, host another program at the same time. This is much more likely to happen in a library or similar facility where you are not paying room rental fees, but the same problems can also occur in a facility where you are paying usage fees. Here you do have some recourse (if you have specified rooms named in your contract), but this is certainly not something you need to deal with the day of a training session.

An ounce of prevention – a trainer's toolbox

So you've followed all the steps discussed thus far and created a wonderful and effective training session, and you're now ready to deliver your training. All that's left to do is show up at your session, right? Almost. Before you turn off your computer, let's talk about backing up your equipment and files. Like a Scout, a good trainer is always prepared. Not unlike a Swiss Army knife full of different tools, you, as a trainer, can readily assemble a tookbox full of ideas and things that you can use to get yourself out of any jams. In taking your show on the road, or presenting in your home location, this preparedness can be crucial to the success of the program. To get a job done right, a professional carries with them their tools of choice, and a trainer is no different. In addition to your Power Point and handouts, you need to bring a few other things with you.

The first thing to 'pack' is extras – be sure to have extra supplies on hand: extra pens, pencils, markers, flipchart pads, name tags, scratch paper, tape, index cards, duct tape, etc. Whatever supplies you plan to use during the course of your training session, be sure to have a toolbox or container stocked with extras. If you are having handouts during the program, whether they are outlines of the entire program or exercises to be completed, bring at least five extra sets of each of the handouts. Sometimes the copier smears a page or someone wants an extra copy of this for their boss, co-worker, etc., so carry a few extra for these times. And a first aid kit won't hurt; you never know when you'll need a Band Aid. For that matter, a small but powerful flashlight can be a life-saver in a power outage in a strange location.

On the high-tech side, you want to bring a long heavy-duty extension cord and either masking or duct tape to tack it down (so you or the participants don't trip!). If you are travelling with your own digital projector, bring extra bulbs, and if you are using the projection equipment in the facility, consider bringing your own as a backup. Projectors are getting smaller and less expensive, so having your own projector to use for presentations is no longer something that is out of reach. The same would hold true for the computer running the presentation software – bring your own laptop as a backup. You should have multiple copies of your presentation saved by different methods such as a memory stick, on your laptop, in your email, and/or saved to an online storage website. You should always have at least two backups of all of your files, just in case. There are several online storage sites available for use after a free registration and they are listed in the resources section at the end of the chapter.

Your presentation may also involve using the internet for showing different websites and you do need to have a backup plan for this also – but have you ever tried to copy or backup the internet? That would take a VERY large memory stick! However, using various screen recording programs you can record the actions on the websites you need to access or demo during the presentation, and if the internet connection or the website is down during your presentation, you can still show the participants what you intended. There are numerous screen recording programs available at little or no cost that are quite easy to use and easy to learn. A few names and websites are included in the resource list at the end of the chapter.

The key thing to remember with the screen recording is that you are not recording this in hopes of winning an Academy Award; it is an emergency backup plan, so if it is not perfect, that's okay. If you happen to click on the wrong spot and need to go back or mistype the URL, that's acceptable. If you need to use this backup plan, chances are that the tension in the room (and your own personal tension level) is running quite high. Making a joke out of a mistake will rapidly diffuse the tension, both for the participants and you. Most times participants are aware of problems as they are occurring and they will tend to root for the problem to be solved, so if there is a solution that works but is less than perfect, they will be accepting.

If you are planning to employ video conferencing, have a backup plan (i.e. a speaker phone and phone connection) in the event the technology doesn't arrive intact or on time, fails at the last minute, or you experience issues with electrical sources. And on a more practical note, check all of your equipment (projectors, DVD player, voice recorders, laptops, stereos, remote controls, etc.) making sure that they work compatibly with one another, are up to date with any upgrades and updates, and that you have plenty of batteries or additional sources of power, and the necessary cords, adapters, power strips and other accoutrements to successfully connect all the pieces of your training plan. If you are travelling, check in with the local tech folks to determine the versions of software the facility is using. Asking them how often they run updates of software is a way to determine how up to date the facility software will be without having to ask directly and possibly offend the staff.

While we have given you ideas on how to handle problems with equipment and the facility, there is still one other area where there might be a problem. What would you do if you are ill the day of the training or if you are travelling and have transportation problems that preclude you from getting to the training session? If you have a co-trainer for the sessions, your co-trainer is your backup and you are your co-trainer's backup. The concept of co-training was discussed earlier in this chapter, so you are aware that you need to be completely familiar with your co-trainer's content and be ready to step in at a moment's notice. If you are not fortunate enough to have a co-trainer, then the session would need to be postponed. If this is the case, try to remember that this is not the end of the world; there are a few reasons that a session might need to be postponed, such as dangerous weather conditions, illness, or something as simple as a power or utility (heat or A/C) outage. The session only needs to be postponed, not cancelled; it can be presented at a later date.

We hope that the tips and tricks presented in this chapter help to ease your mind prior to your training sessions. Being able to relax prior to training is important. If you are very nervous and uptight, this will translate to your participants and thus set the mood for your training session. A small amount of trainer nerves are the norm for any trainer, so try and relax prior to the training. Look over your notes, take some deep cleansing breaths, take a short walk down the hall – anything that burns off some excess energy and makes you feel more relaxed. At this point – you *are* prepared and ready to present a great training session – relax, enjoy it, and have fun. The participants will definitely follow your lead on this attitude and have a great time also.

Useful links

Equipment

Dell M109S On-the-Go Projector – *http://www.dell.com*

Capture software

CamStudio – *http://camstudio.org/*
Jing – *http://www.techsmith.com/jing/*
Capture Fox – *https://addons.mozilla.org/en-US/firefox/addon/ capture-fox/*

Online presentation storage

SlideShare – *http://www.slideshare.net/*
SlideRocket – *http://www.sliderocket.com/*
Dropbox – *https://www.dropbox.com/*

References

Cook, L. and Friend, M. (2004) *Co-teaching: Principles, Practices, and Pragmatics*. In the Quarterly Special Education Meeting April 29, 2004. Symposium conducted at the New Mexico Public Education Department, Albuquerque, NM.

Villa, R., Thousand, J. and Nevin, A. (2008) *A Guide to Co-teaching: Practical Tips for Facilitating Student Learning*. Thousand Oaks, CA: Corwin Press.

Part 4
Training completed! What next?

9

Keeping current

Abstract: What you learn in this book is just the beginning of the learning you will do as you progress in your training career. Continuing education is important for your career as a library professional and library trainer. This chapter will address the reasons for keeping current in the field, and various methods of acquiring new and diverse information that will enhance your training abilities.

Key words: continuing professional development, social media, personal learning network, distance education, Web 2.0, self-directed learning.

Why continuing education?

The field of librarianship is ever expanding and changing, from exploding Internet and media technologies to ever-diverse patron groups with increasingly complex information needs. Library professionals need to be as savvy as the clients they serve, and the most productive and effective way for librarians to keep up with these changes is to seek out professional development opportunities. Librarians and library staff members owe it to their clients, and to themselves as competent professionals, to remain abreast of trends and developments in the field. This is particularly pertinent for those library staff members charged with teaching and training their colleagues and patrons.

Hopefully, you have gained some new information and ideas as a result of reading this text. However, the lessons provided only scratch the surface of the art of training and presenting. Training and presenting is an ongoing practice and set of skills that need continual tweaking and development.

Continuing education/professional development

Learning and education do not cease with the attainment of a Masters Degree in Library Science; quite the opposite, the degree is only the beginning of a librarian's education. Weingand states that,

> the shelf life of a degree is approximately three years and declining. Maintaining competence and learning new skills must be at the top of every professional's 'To Do' list. It is an ethical responsibility, to be sure, but also one that is pragmatic and critical for career success ... Continuing professional education is no longer an option, it is a requirement of professional practice. (Weingand, 1999: 201)

Weingand goes on to define continuing professional education (CPE) as 'Education that takes place once professional qualification is achieved, with the intent of maintaining competence and/or learning new skills' (ibid.).

As essential as CPE is, there are several fundamental dilemmas that will keep it from uniformly benefitting the field of librarianship. As a point of entry, the field of librarianship requires a Masters degree, and, with rare exceptions (some public librarians and school librarians),

librarians do not need any form of licensure, certification, or credentials to assume professional positions. Therefore, with no requirements to uphold and maintain, CPE for librarians is voluntary. Certain specialties of librarianship, and their associated professional organizations (for example medical librarians and special librarians), offer regimented CPE and credentialing programs for their members; however, while such credentials may be desirable to certain employers, they are still optional endeavors and are not necessary for employment.

Two other significant dilemmas facing library and information science (LIS) CPE are the absence of a central repository or clearinghouse for educational offerings, and the lack of quality control mechanisms to govern said offerings. Because CPE is not a professional requirement, there are no regulations in place regarding the development and offering of CPE programs; any school or agency can offer CPE programs for librarians. As a consequence of not having a central agency regulating LIS CPE, there are no standards or quality control measures in place. Varlejs states that 'Quality control in the LIS CPE field is very rare, if it exists at all' (Varlejs, 2002: 235). Issues of quality control and a central repository for CPE offerings are a frequent topic of discussion at library conferences, most notably the American Library Association's (ALA) Congress on Professional Education (COPE) summits, held in 2000 and 2001.

COPE garnered participation from all major professional library organizations, and the meeting's recommendations included establishing an independent and comprehensive clearinghouse for CPE offerings, establishing congruence between CPE and library conference offerings, taking direction from other professions who mandate CPE from their practitioners (Varlejs, 2001), and encouraging LIS educators to infuse more of their research into professional practice, and to:

> Inculcate the lifelong learning ethos, together with the skills to become an effective independent, self-directed learner. ... It is crucial, however, to make students recognize that they are only at the beginning of their learning, and that they must accept responsibility personally for continuing their own professional development. (Varlejs, 2003: 371)

The ALA/APA's Continuing Library Education Network and Exchange (CLENE), and the International Federation of Library Associations and Institutions' (IFLA) Continuing Professional Development and Workplace Learning Section are active organizations that have continued to discuss the issues and recommendations brought forth by COPE, but it appears that no substantial and lasting progress has been made as of 2008, most likely due to the huge financial and stakeholders coordination such an endeavor requires. Mayfield summarizes the current state of affairs by stating:

> No single organization, institution, or agency could marshal the resources needed to address the agenda. A collaborate effort is required, an effort that itself may contain the seeds of the development of an integrated, holistic framework for education and training beyond the classroom. (Mayfield, 1993: 430)

With the aforementioned issues surrounding formal CPE, there have been new developments on the LIS CPE landscape, notably online professional development. With the rapid development of Web 2.0/social software tools, many librarians are supplementing, and even substituting, formal CPE for online tools such as blogs, wikis and social networking communities. These online tools are especially attractive because they are free, do not require dedicated blocks of time or travel, and they offer the potential to create lasting learning communities that foster ongoing professional development. Certainly, the same quality control issues that plague formal/in person CPE apply to online CPE, and the same considerations employed with online LIS education are applicable to online CPE development.

Web 2.0

Web 2.0/social networking software applications (Abram, 2008; Technorati, 2008; Anderson, 2007; Vickery and Wunsch-Vincent, 2007; Boulos and Wheelert, 2007; Laning et al., 2005; Bar-llan, 2004) continue to grow in popularity and are proving themselves to be worthwhile for more than just purely social uses. These tools, which are billed to be huge proponents of interactivity and community building, seem a natural extension for LIS CPE. Abram asserts,

> Web 2.0 is ultimately about a social phenomenon –
> not just about networked social experiences, but about
> the distribution and creation of Web content itself,
> 'characterized by open communication, decentralization
> of authority, freedom to share and reuse, and the
> market as a conversation.' It moves the Web experience
> into a place that more closely resembles an academic
> learning collaboration environment than an information
> delivery and e-commerce vehicle. (Abram, 2008: 20)

Figures 9.1 and 9.2 provide very basic definitions of Web 2.0 and some of the most popular applications being used for online LIS CPE.

The emphasis on interactivity and community building are the qualities that make Web 2.0 tools especially applicable to LIS CPE and will make this method of learning successful. In particular, three concepts, self-directed learning, electronic culture, and communities of practice, contribute to our understanding of how online CPE with social software tools is a viable and beneficial alternative for librarians.

Figure 9.1   Web 2.0 social software

WEB 2.0

Web 2.0/Social Software

- "A huge range of tools ... the features that many of them share are that they are hosted remotely, they facilitate sharing and communication, they allow users to add content and they are easy to use" (Secker, 2008, p. 216).
- "Web 2.0 is about the more human aspects of interactivity. It is about conversations, interpersonal networking, personalization and individualism. It is focused on content in the context of people, workplaces, markets, community, and learning" (Abram, 2008, p. 20).

Examples of Social Software

- Typically free services, social software includes blogs, wikis, media sharing (i.e., flickr, You Tube, slideshare, podcasting), mashups, virtual worlds, RSS feeds, streaming media, folksonomies, tagging, social networking sites, chat, IM, and even collaborative filters such as amazon. com's readers' recommendations.

Figure 9.2 Web 2.0 examples

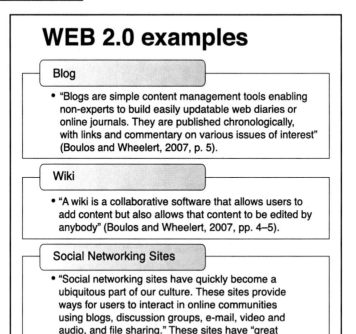

WEB 2.0 examples

Blog

- "Blogs are simple content management tools enabling non-experts to build easily updatable web diaries or online journals. They are published chronologically, with links and commentary on various issues of interest" (Boulos and Wheelert, 2007, p. 5).

Wiki

- "A wiki is a collaborative software that allows users to add content but also allows that content to be edited by anybody" (Boulos and Wheelert, 2007, pp. 4–5).

Social Networking Sites

- "Social networking sites have quickly become a ubiquitous part of our culture. These sites provide ways for users to interact in online communities using blogs, discussion groups, e-mail, video and audio, and file sharing." These sites have "great potential as an educational tool, especially for professional development and building professional connections (Rosenfeld, 2008, p. 60).

Building online learning communities

Self-directed learning

Self-directed learning is a concept borrowed from the field of adult education, and really speaks to the motivation of librarians seeking CPE, particularly in the unregulated and time-unconscious environment of the Internet. Self-directed learning is simply defined as learning that is 'informal, self-initiated, independently conducted, and integrated into individuals' daily work' (Varlejs, 1996: 2). This is a most appropriate description of how library professionals might incorporate blog and wiki reading, and participation in online communities into their daily practice. Formal CPE is not to be negated or disparaged in any way, but is not always appropriate or available, because of various time and financial constraints. It appears that their professional development activities are not influenced by the amount of release time, financial assistance, or other support provided in their work setting. Rather, they may be motivated by factors inherent in the nature of their work and by expectations of performance imposed by employers and clients. Or, perhaps, an ingrained affinity for learning may be the best explanation (Varlejs, 1999: 63–4).

Varlejs (1996), a library scholar whose body of work has contributed greatly to the field's knowledge of self-directed learning and CPE endeavors, reported that a significant number of library professionals belonging to the American Library Association engage in self-directed learning.[1] Varlejs also points out that self-directed learning is not to be conflated with formal CPE, formal learning associated with the pursuit of an academic degree, or current awareness activities (i.e., reading a professional article to acquire information about a specific event, trend, or tool).

Electronic culture: collective intelligence and knowledge communities

Mass media scholars Jenkins (2006), and Kahn and Kellner (2005) contribute to our understanding of how technology and media can foster and facilitate online culture and knowledge communities, which are especially pertinent when teaching and learning online. Jenkins (2006) mentions two interesting concepts, collective intelligence and knowledge communities. Collective intelligence is described by stating, 'None of us can know everything; each of us knows something; and we can put the pieces together if we pool our resources and combine our skills. Collective intelligence can be seen as an alternative source of media power' (Jenkins, 2006: 4).

I would argue that collective intelligence can also be seen as an alternative source of *educational* power. For example, in online LIS education, bulletin boards are often used to supplement and/or replace traditional face-to-face conversations. In this way, each learner has the opportunity to contribute their opinions, experiences, and interpretations to a common area, thereby shaping the learning experience and overall understanding. In effect, collective intelligence contributes to the formation of knowledge communities.

Referring more specifically to social software applications, Boulos and Wheelert (2007) feel that these technologies foster collective intelligence and decrease isolation, and have the 'potential to promote active and engaged learning, where participants themselves construct their own knowledge through social interaction and exploration. Learning becomes an active process in which peers collaborate equally so none might dominate the interaction' (Boulos and Wheelert, 2007: 18).

About knowledge communities, Jenkins says that 'knowledge communities form around mutual intellectual interests; their members work together to forge new knowledge often in realms where no traditional expertise exists; the pursuit of and assessment of knowledge is at once communal and adversarial' (Jenkins, 2006: 20).

Kahn and Kellner discuss blogs and wikis, which are enormously popular, powerful, and excellent examples of social networking and knowledge communities. If the WWW was about forming a global network of interlocking, informative websites, blogs make the idea of a dynamic network of ongoing debate, dialogue, and commentary come alive and so emphasize the interpretation and dissemination of alternative information to a heightened degree (Kahn and Kellner 2005: 88). While specifically discussing blogs and wikis in a political environment, there are many examples of blogs and wikis being used to facilitate communities in all types of specialized communities (ibid.: 91). These tools can be extended to include online LIS CPE communities, several examples of which are briefly presented below. While beneficial, care must be taken not to allow online knowledge communities to completely substitute for, or supersede other methods of communication and interaction.

Communities of practice

Another related concept, this time from the management literature, is communities of practice. The concept, developed by Wenger (1998, 2001), is not dissimilar from the concepts of collective intelligence and knowledge communities. Wenger defines a community of practice by stating,

> Members of a community are informally bound by what they do together – from engaging in lunchtime discussions to solving difficult problems – and by what they have learned through their mutual engagement in these activities. A community of practice is thus different from a community of interest of a geographical community, neither of which implies a shared practice. (Wenger, 1998: 2).

Wenger continues by specifying three distinct dimensions of a community of practice: they are joint enterprises, meaning they are created and maintained by their members, they feature mutual engagement, meaning all members come together to form a social entity, and the members have a shared repertoire of resources and sensibilities that have been communally developed over time (ibid.). Wenger does caution that communities of practice should take care not to become insular, rather they should remain dynamic and fluid entities which constantly renew their learning, 'for while the core is the center of expertise, radically new insights often arise at the boundary between communities' (ibid.: 6).

Personal learning networks (PLNs)

Personal learning networks build upon the notions of collective knowledge, communities of practice and follow up on how to actually form such learning communities. Built upon the theories of social learning and connectivism,[2] PLNs consist of a learner and the contacts and colleagues with whom they surround themselves. These networks need not occur face-to-face or in real time, nor does the learner have to personally know their knowledge collaborators. PLNs are often specifically devoted to professional learning and development, and are keen to apply technology which makes them as local or global in reach as the learner desires. 'Including technology and connection making as learning activities begins to move learning theories into a digital age. We can no longer personally experience and acquire learning that we need to act. We derive our competence from forming connections' (Siemens, 2005).

Professional development 2.0: examples

The concepts of self-directed learning, electronic culture and communities of practice frame and extend our understanding of how Web 2.0 tools can be successful vehicles for LIS CPE. The consistent and interactive nature of these tools allows learning to be more robust and enduring than a singular meeting of class session. Examples of social software applications being used for LIS CPE are blogs, wikis and social networking communities. Blogs are perhaps the most prolific and well known applications being used for CPE (Technorati, 2008; Laning et al., 2005; Bar-Ilan, 2004), because they are frequently free of charge, potential authors do not need to know programming languages or HTML to update and maintain their pages, and it is easy to keep blogs up to date.

Blogs, which began appearing in 1997,

> can alleviate information overload by helping the reader filter the important news in any domain . . . the reader can use blogs as a professional development tool to stay abreast in the LIS field, and follow new resources, technological advances, research, vendor activity, new materials, conferences, and job postings. (Laning et al., 2005: 165)

When Laning et al. wrote this, there were over 400 blogs related to LIS issues and services; that number has surely increased since 2005, and it has been written that blogs have exploded in the last 10 years, from 23 blogs in 1999 to 10 million in 2004 (Bar-Ilan, 2004: 119), and to well over 78 million in 2008 (Technorati, 2008).

Wikis are also being increasingly used for collaborative work, and are sometimes preferred because they allow the creation of more traditional, or linear, pages and documents. Unlike blogs, wikis generally have a *history* function, which allows previous versions to be examined, and a *rollback* function, which restores previous versions. Proponents of the power of wikis cite the ease of use (even playfulness) of the tools, their extreme flexibility and open access as some of the many reasons why they are useful for group working (Anderson, 2007: 8).

Social networking sites are also growing in popularity, as they incorporate many social software tools into one platform. Social networking sites 'enable users to connect to friends and colleagues, to send e-mails and instant messages, to blog, to meet new people and to post personal information profiles. Profiles include photos, video, images, audio, and blogs' (Vickery and Wunsch-Vincent, 2007: 38).

Perhaps among the most popular social media tools for developing and maintain PLNs is Twitter. Twitter, the popular micro blogging service that requires posters to convey messages in 140 characters or less, allows access to a wide variety of educational and professorial colleagues and resources. Posts often contain links and citations, and there are many chats and discussions that are linked together by designated hash tags. The result is a 24/7, and in many instances instantaneous, network of likeminded people with similar academic interests. These short bursts of information are convenient. A learner could post a question about training and presenting to their Twitter PLN and within hours be provided with a wealth of tips and tricks, further reading and information.

Another example of social networking sites are Ning networks, which allow anyone to create a social network, based on any interest, similar to the ease with which people create blogs. Ning networks have an increased air of individuality and customization possibilities.

Social networking sites have quickly become a ubiquitous part of our culture. These sites provide ways for users to interact in online communities using blogs, discussion groups, e-mail, video and audio, and file sharing. Ning is one example of a growing number of sites that create a social network for a specific audience around practically any interest, group, or activity. Ning has great potential as an education tool, especially for professional development and building profession connections (Rosenfeld, 2008: 60).

Technology and media have changed the face of LIS education and extended its reach worldwide, and with these new technologies and opportunities come new considerations about communication and interaction. From a personal perspective, the most effective learning situations, face-to-face and online, are those that have included significant interaction and discussion with colleagues, in an environment where students are co-creators of knowledge with their peers and the instructor. Although this type of learning environment takes significant planning and effort to create and maintain in an online environment, it is certainly worthwhile and will further benefit online LIS continuing professional education.

Notes

1. Varlejs' dissertation study drew from a random sample of 39,900 ALA members, resulting in 849 survey recipients. Of those recipients, 521, or 58%, participated in self-directed learning.

2. Siemens (2005) defines connectivism as "the integration of principles explored by chaos, network, and complexity and self-organization theories. Learning is a process that occurs within nebulous environments of shifting core elements – not entirely under the control of the individual. Learning (defined as actionable knowledge) can reside outside of ourselves (within an organization or a

database), is focused on connecting specialized information sets, and the connections that enable us to learn more are more important than our current state of knowing.

Useful links and further reading

Blogs and Internet sites

Dave Paradi's PowerPoint blog – *http://pptideas.blogspot. com/*

The Educator's PLN – *http://edupln.ning.com/*

The Eloquent Woman: Inspiration, ideas and information to help women with public speaking techniques, eloquence and confidence – *http://eloquentwoman.blogspot.com/*

Presentation Zen – *http://www.presentationzen.com/*

Prezi – *http://prezi.com/index/*

Sacha Chua: living an awesome life – *http://sachachua.com/ blog*

Six Minutes: speaking and presentations blog – *http:// sixminutes.dlugan.com/*

SlideShare – *http://www.slideshare.net/*

Speaking about Presenting – *http://speakingaboutpresenting. com/*

Speak Schmeak – *http://coachlisab.blogspot.com/*

TED: Ideas worth spreading – *http://blog.ted.com/*

Teacher Librarian – *http://www.teacherlibrarian.ning.com*

Twitter – *http://twitter.com/*

Further reading

Duarte, N. (2010) *Resonate: Present Visual Stories that Transform Audiences.* Sebastopol, CA: O'Reilly Media.

Duarte, N. (2008) *Slideology: The Art and Science of Creating Great Presentations*. Sebastopol, CA: O'Reilly Media.

Pike, R. (2003) *Creative Training Techniques Handbook: Tips, Tactics, and How-to's for Delivering Effective Training*. Amherst, MA: Human Resource Development Press.

Reynolds, G. (2010) *The Naked Presenter: Delivering Powerful Presentations with or without Slides*. Berkeley, CA: New Riders Press.

Reynolds, G. (2009) *Presentation Zen Design: Simple Design Principles and Techniques to Enhance Your Presentations*. Berkeley, CA: New Riders Press.

Reynolds, G. (2008) *Presentation Zen: Simple Ideas on Presentation Design and Delivery*. Berkeley, CA: New Riders Press.

Terrell, S. (2010) 23 resources about personal learning networks (PLNs), Retrieved March 1, 2011, from *http://teacherbootcamp.edublogs.org/2010/05/09/16-resources-about-personal-learning-networks-plns/*

References

Abram, S. (2008) Social libraries: The librarian 2.0 phenomenon. *Library Resources & Technical Services*, 52(2), 19–22.

Anderson, P. (2007) What is Web 2.0? Ideas, technologies and implications for Education. *JISC Technology & Standards Watch*. Retrieved November 10, 2008, from *http://www.jisc.ac.uk/media/documents/techwatch/tsw0701b.pdf*

Bar-Ilan, J. (2004) Blogarians: A new breed of librarians. *Proceedings of the 67th ASIS&T Annual Meeting*, 41, 119–28.

Boulos, M.N.K. and Wheelert, S. (2007) The emerging Web 2.0 social software: An enabling suite of sociable technologies in health and health care education. *Health Information and Libraries Journal*, 24, 2–23.

Jenkins, H. (2006) *Convergence Culture*. New York: NYU Press.

Kahn, R. and Kellner, D.M. (2005) Oppositional politics and the internet: A critical/reconstructive approach. *Cultural Politics*, 1(**1**), 75–100.

Laning, M., Lavallee-Welch, C. and Smith, M. (2005) Frontiers of effort: Librarians and professional development blogs. *Journal of Library Administration*, 43(**3/4**), 161–79.

Mayfield, M.K. (1993) Beyond the classroom: self-direction in professional learning. *Bulletin of the Medical Library Association*, 81(4), 425–32.

Rosenfeld, E. (2008) Expanding your professional network with Nings. *Teacher Librarian*, 35(3), 60.

Siemens, G. (2005) Connectivism: A learning theory for the digital age. *International Journal of Instructional Technology and Distance Learning*, 2(1), available at *http://www.itdl.org/Journal/Jan_05/article01.htm*

Technorati (2008) *State of the Blogosphere/2008*. Retrieved November 20, 2008, from Technorati's web site: *http://technorati.com/blogging/state-of-the-blogosphere/*

Varlejs, J. (2002) Quality control and assurance for continuing professional education. In *Continuing Professional Education for the Information Society: The Fifth World Conference of Continuing Professional Education for the Library and Information Science Professions*, Saur, Germany (pp. 232–4). The Hague, Netherlands: International Federation of Library Associations and Institutions.

Varlejs, J. (1999) Profile of the academic librarian as self-directed learner. In P.O. Libutti (ed.), *Librarians as*

Learners, Librarians as Teachers: The Diffusion of Internet Expertise in the Academic Library. Chicago, IL: Association of College & Research Libraries (pp. 51–65).

Varlejs, J. (1996) *Librarians' Self-Directed Continuing Professional Learning.* Ph.D. dissertation, The University of Wisconsin at Madison, WI. Retrieved November 21, 2008, from ProQuest Dissertations and Theses Database (Publication No. AAT 9622535).

Vickery, G. and Wunsch-Vincent, S. (2007) *Participative Web and User-Created Content: Web 2.0, Wikis and Social Networking.* Paris: Organization for Economic Co-operation and Development.

Weingand, D.E. (1999) Describing the elephant: What is continuing professional education. *IFLA Journal,* 26(3), 198–202.

Wenger, E. (2001), Communities of practice. In N. J. Smelser and P. B. Baltes (eds), *International Encyclopedia of the Social & Behavioral Sciences.* Amsterdam: Elsevier Science (pp. 2339–42).

Wenger, E. (1998), Communities of practice: learning as a social system. *The Systems Thinker,* 9(5), 1–5.

10

Keeping connected

Abstract: A successful training session will hopefully be effective and a source of new professional contacts and networking. In order to nurture and maintain the new community, plan on keeping connected with your participants. Share news, tips, follow-up opportunities, and other such relevant information. This chapter discusses ways to keep participants connected to the training content, each other, and the trainers. Advantages and disadvantages of each method are discussed. Suggested resources are also provided for your consideration.

Key words: listserv, blog, wiki, e-newsletters, online discussion groups.

Congratulations! It's been a long road, but the training is finally completed. Evaluations have been positive and the participants are beginning to integrate the concepts into their work life. But how can we keep them moving forward, keep them thinking of the concepts learned in the sessions, keep them connected as a group to allow them to serve as resources to each other? There are many different to keep in contact with the participants of training sessions and your choice of which to use, or none at all, depends on the content of the training session and the time you have available to devote to this task. Let's take a look at the more popular means: listservs, blogs and wikis, e-newsletters, and online discussion groups. Some of these methods may also be used to contact participants after the training is completed to perform behavior-level evaluations.

Listserv

Setting up an email listserv is possible if you are part of a large organization or consortium that has an e-mail client with this capability. If you are not, there is free software available for downloading that will provide this capability. Paid software is also available. Once the list is set up, you and the participants may post items of interest, issues and topics for discussion to the list. There are advantages to using a listserv to keep in contact, one being that messages are delivered to the subscriber's inbox and they see at least the subject line and will proceed to read the message if their interest is peaked. Messages can be grouped into a digest or filtered by the user into a folder for later reading so the intrusiveness factor can be controlled by the recipient. Another advantage is that you only need to post a message when you have something to say; a web presence needs to be updated on a regular basis or it will appear outdated. Even if you do not have the software or are tech-savvy enough to set one up, a simple e-mail distribution list can suffice. Disadvantages to an e-mail listserv discussion are keeping track of the tread of discussion and also having people 'reply to all' on the e-mail if you are using a simple email distribution list. Long and popular discussion threads can become quite drawn out and hard to follow when many people are posting at the same time.

E-newsletters

E-newsletters are simply newsletters delivered to various recipients via e-mail. There are several free programs available for downloading, or you could produce a version as a word processing document and send it to your list via email. The main advantage to an e-newsletter is that it can be produced and sent for free to as many people as you wish. As with listserv messages, the recipient has the choice to view or discard the email, so the level of intrusiveness is low. Depending how often you might wish to reach out to the training participants, you may not have enough information to fill a newsletter on a regular basis, so the document may appear to be repetitive or forced full of information. Also, you lose any possibility of the recipients being able to begin a discussion amongst themselves as the newsletter is static with no area for a discussion. You could invite the participants to send in questions/ideas for topics in future newsletters, but any immediate interaction between them is not possible.

Blogs and wikis

Blogs and wikis are basically websites that are easily designed and updated by the average computer user. Several free services are available to design and host your webpage. Getting started is quite easy and updating is truly a breeze. Participants can submit a comment to any posting and it either gets posted immediately or waits for approval from you (as the owner of the blog). The ability for the participants to interact with you and each other is high and even novice computer users do not have problems successfully posting comments. There are, however, a couple of disadvantages to using blogs and wikis. They are readily available on the World Wide Web, so not only can anyone see the discussions, the participants may again fear recrimination by their supervisor and therefore might not speak freely in the discussions. And here again you have the issue of content; if you don't update or produce new content on a regular basis, the page quickly becomes stale and eventually your participants will stop coming to the page. Lastly, and perhaps most important – this is yet another place the participant needs to visit to obtain updated information or assistance. With the listserv and the e-newsletter the information is delivered to them, eliminating the need to remember to go elsewhere.

Online discussion groups

Online discussion groups can be formed in various software platforms the most common being Google, Yahoo! and Facebook. All will have similar functions, such as being able to post topics for discussion, allow participants to post answers and pose new queries, and allow for mass email to be sent to all members. Some will allow document sharing and posting of pictures, so it might be best to think about in what direction(s) you want the group to head before deciding upon a software platform. Facebook has the disadvantage of needing participants to have a Facebook account to give them access to the group. While it may be hard to fathom, there still are some people that do not have a Facebook account, nor do they want one. Most other software simply requires the members of the group to have some sort of email account. All systems will obtain and keep on file some personal information on each participant (mainly name and email address) so this is also something to consider if you are thinking of starting a group for your training participants.

There are numerous online means of keeping connected with the past participants of your training sessions. This can be advantageous for any number of reasons, but keeping them moving forward on the concepts presented and learned in the training session is the most important. The amount of work required to set up and maintain a connection can vary, so looking carefully at the different options is definitely something that should be done. Whatever method is chosen, you will have the problem common to all methods: How do I get people to read and react to what I've sent/posted? The answer is not an easy one because it may differ from person to person and course to course, but as a general rule keep your posts/emails short, sweet and to the point. Use words that will catch people's interest in titles, subject lines, and other prominent areas. Once you have peaked their interest, perhaps they will at least scan through the entire posting/ email and may even post a reply.

While this discussion presents a dark view of participants' reaction to your reconnection with them following the training sessions, most likely this will be far from the actual reaction. Most participants are very happy with their trainers and actually enjoy hearing from them post-training. They will remember the sessions and the key concepts presented and learned, so you have done well in your job as their trainer and can rest assured that this is the case – even if they do not answer.

Useful links

Listservs

Mailman – *http://www.gnu.org/software/mailman/index.html*
L-Soft – *http://www.lsoft.com/products/emaillist.asp*

Wikis

PBworks – *http://pbworks.com/*
Wikispaces – *http://www.wikispaces.com/*

Blogs

Blogger – *www.blogger.com*
WordPress – *http://wordpress.com/*

E-newsletters

http://mailchimp.com/

Discussion groups

Google Groups – *http://groups.google.com/*
Yahoo! Groups – *http://groups.yahoo.com/*

Afterword

We truly hope that you've found this book helpful and that you now feel as though you have acquired the skills necessary to plan, design, conduct, and refine an effective training session. Now that you know all the components of a good training session, you will be able to successfully train individual patrons at a service point, teach a group of students how to use the library's resources, prepare a session for your organization's annual retreat, give a workshop at a professional conference, and plan a multi-day, multi-session professional development workshop.

Training, whether done individually, or in tandem with colleagues or a cadre of volunteers, can be remarkably beneficial and rewarding to your constituents and to you as you continue to develop as a library professional. We wish you success and enjoyment as you embark on your path as a library instructor and trainer!

Index

CPSIA information can be obtained at www.ICGtesting.com
Printed in the USA
LVOW071757200412

278533LV00001B/5/P